1,000,000 Books

are available to read at

www.ForgottenBooks.com

Read online
Download PDF
Purchase in print

ISBN 978-0-282-92043-2
PIBN 10867548

This book is a reproduction of an important historical work. Forgotten Books uses state-of-the-art technology to digitally reconstruct the work, preserving the original format whilst repairing imperfections present in the aged copy. In rare cases, an imperfection in the original, such as a blemish or missing page, may be replicated in our edition. We do, however, repair the vast majority of imperfections successfully; any imperfections that remain are intentionally left to preserve the state of such historical works.

Forgotten Books is a registered trademark of FB &c Ltd.
Copyright © 2018 FB &c Ltd.
FB &c Ltd, Dalton House, 60 Windsor Avenue, London, SW19 2RR.
Company number 08720141. Registered in England and Wales.

For support please visit www.forgottenbooks.com

1 MONTH OF FREE READING

at
www.ForgottenBooks.com

By purchasing this book you are eligible for one month membership to ForgottenBooks.com, giving you unlimited access to our entire collection of over 1,000,000 titles via our web site and mobile apps.

To claim your free month visit:
www.forgottenbooks.com/free867548

* Offer is valid for 45 days from date of purchase. Terms and conditions apply.

English
Français
Deutsche
Italiano
Español
Português

www.forgottenbooks.com

Mythology Photography **Fiction** Fishing Christianity **Art** Cooking Essays **Buddhism** Freemasonry Medicine **Biology** Music **Ancient Egypt** Evolution Carpentry Physics Dance Geology **Mathematics** Fitness Shakespeare **Folklore** Yoga Marketing **Confidence** Immortality Biographies Poetry **Psychology** Witchcraft Electronics Chemistry History **Law** Accounting **Philosophy** Anthropology Alchemy Drama Quantum Mechanics Atheism Sexual Health **Ancient History Entrepreneurship** Languages Sport Paleontology Needlework Islam **Metaphysics** Investment Archaeology Parenting Statistics Criminology **Motivational**

VOL. XXXV. JANUARY, 1927 NO. 1

SCENE ON THE DAVIS FARM NEAR SMYRNA, TENN.

Stewart's Creek borders the Sam Davis home place in Rutherford County, Tenn., and the scene here given shows the creek just west of the old house where Sam Davis was born and lived his short life. The State will be asked to purchase the house and lands as a memorial to Tennessee's boy hero of the sixties, the plan being to make it a memorial museum and park. See page 5.

BOOKS WORTH WHILE.

To those who are interested in making a collection of worth-while books on Southern and Confederate history the following list will present some valuable offerings:

Messages and Papers of the Confederacy. Compiled by Hon. James D. Richardson. Two volumes; cloth bound.................$7 00
Origin of the Late War. Traced from the beginning of the Constitution to the revolt of the Southern States. By George Lunt................. 4 00
Southern Generals: Who They Are and What They Have Done, By a Virginian, 1865..................... 4 00
Life of Gen. R. E. Lee. By Gen. A. L. Long. Good copy; cloth.......... 5 00
Life and Campaigns of Stonewall Jackson. By Dr. R. L. Dabney......... 4 00
Life of Gen. A. S. Johnston. By Col. William Preston Johnston.., ... 4 50
Life of Jefferson Davis. By Frank H. Alfriend..........;........ 4 00
Memorial Volume of Jefferson Davis. By Dr. J. William Jones.......... 4 00
Shelby and His Men. By John N. Edwards. Good copy; scarce.......... 6 00
Destruction and Reconstruction. By Gen. Richard Taylor............... 4 00
Reminiscences of the Civil War. By Gen. John B. Gordon............. 4 00
France and the Confederate Navy. By John Bigelow.................... 3 50
Service Afloat During the War between the States, By Admiral Raphael Semmes. Good copy; original edition:..................... 7 50
Service Afloat and Ashore During the War with Mexico. By Lieut. Raphael Semmes. 1851.................... 6 00
Recollections of a Naval Life. Cruise of the Sumter and Alabama. By John McIntosh Kell........................ 4 00
Cruise of the Shenandoah. Last Confederate vessel afloat, By Cornelius Hunt, one of her officers..........................., ... 3 50
Raphael Semmes. By Colyer Meriwether............................. 2 00
With Saber and Scalpel. By Dr. John Allen Wyeth. Nice copy; cloth..... 4 50
Hammer and Rapier. By John Esten Cooke........................... 1 50
Reminiscences of Peace and War. By Mrs. Roger Pryor..............'.. 3 00
Four Years Under Marse Robert. By Major Stiles...................... 3 50

LEADING ARTICLES IN THIS NUMBER.

	PAGE
U. C. V. Interests...........................	3
Memorial to Sam David of Tennessee..................................	5
General Lee's Letter to Lord Acton............'........................	6
Abolition: Northern and Southern Views and Plans. By Mrs. Texa Bowen Williams........................	7
Armories of the Confederacy. By Richard D. Steuart..................	9
Forrest's Wonderful Achievements. By Capt. James Dinkins............	10
Signers of the Declaration of Independence............................	13
When General Mulligan Was Killed. By I. G. Bradwell..................	14
Last of C. S. Ordnance Department. By Joseph R. Haw................	15
South Carolina's Representatives in the Confederate Congress. By Mrs. A. A. Woodson.......................	16
Experiences of a War-Time Girl, By Mrs. John P. Sellman..............	19
When Christmas Came to Journey's End. By Beatrice Kent............	20
November on an Old Battle Field. (Poem.) By Virginia Lucas...........	23
The Service Cross. (Poem.) By Catherine C. Everett..................	31
The Ideal of a State. (Poem.) By Sir William Jones....................	37
A Confederate Cemetery. (Poem.)...................................	38
Departments: Last Roll..	24
U. D. C...........................	28
C, S. M. A...	34
S. C. V...	36

Capt. J. W. Matthews, of Alvon, W. Va., one of the survivors of the "Immortal Six Hundred," and now in his eighty-eighty year, renews his subscription for two years more. He was in the war from start to finish except when in prison. He commanded Company I, 25th Virginia Infantry. He is anxious to get a copy of the book on "The Immortal Six Hundred," and will appreciate hearing from anyone who has this book for sale.

Miss Bess Barbor, 211 Park Avenue, Princeton, W. Va., would like to hear from anyone who served with Ben P. Grigsby, of Company I, 24th Virginia Regiment, Pickett's Division.

J. A. JOEL & CO.

SILK AND BUNTING FLAGS AND BANNERS
U. S., CONFEDERATE, AND STATE FLAGS
SPECIAL FLAGS AND BANNERS MADE TO ORDER AT SHORT NOTICE

147 Fulton Street
New York, N. Y.

A. G. Hunter, 26 Kimberley Avenue, Springfield, Mass., is trying to get his father's record as a Confederate soldier so that he may be able to join the Sons of Confederate Veterans. His father, William Griswold Hunter, was at school at Morristown, Pa., at the time the war opened, but his home was in North Carolina. He enlisted as a schoolboy in 1862, and served under Gen. Joseph E. Johnston and others to the end. His enlistment may have been from North Carolina.

E. W. Hefner, clerk of the Braxton County Court, Flatwoods, W. Va., wishes to get some information of Company G, 62nd Virginia Regiment, with which his father, S. C. Hefner, served as first lieutenant. He wishes some data on the personnel of the company.

Some time ago, J. E. Deupree, of Ravenna, Tex., wrote to the VETERAN of a negro man who had been sent from his Texas home to join his young master in the Confederate army east of the Mississippi River, but who was lost when trying to find him. Comrade Deupree hoped that some one who had come in contact with the negro would remember it and write to him. Strange to say, he did get response from some lady in Alabama who remembered that Rube had come to her home during the war, and he was in search of his master. As the lady's name and address have been lost, he hopes that she will see this notice and write to him again, which he will appreciate.

The haughty Englishman was endeavoring to impress the importance of his family upon his guide in the Scottish Highlands.

"My ancestors," he exclaimed, with a theatrical gesture, "have had the right to bear arms for the last three hundred years."

"Hoot, mon," cried the Scot, "my ancestors have had the right to bare legs for the last two thousand years."—*Canadian-American.*

Confederate Veteran

PUBLISHED MONTHLY IN THE INTEREST OF CONFEDERATE ASSOCIATIONS AND KINDRED TOPICS.

Entered as second-class matter at the post office at Nashville, Tenn., under act of March 3, 1879.
Acceptance of mailing at special rate of postage provided for in Section 1103, act of October 3, 1917, and authorized on July 5, 1918.
Published by the Trustees of the CONFEDERATE VETERAN, Nashville, Tenn.

OFFICIALLY REPRESENTS:
UNITED CONFEDERATE VETERANS,
UNITED DAUGHTERS OF THE CONFEDERACY,
CONFEDERATED SOUTHERN MEMORIAL ASSOCIATION,
SONS OF CONFEDERATE VETERANS.

Though men deserve, they may not win, success;
The brave will honor the brave, vanquished none the less.

| PRICE $1.50 PER YEAR. SINGLE COPY, 15 CENTS. | VOL. XXXV. | NASHVLLE, TENN., JANUARY, 1927. | No. 1. | S. A. CUNNINGHAM FOUNDER. |

UNITED CONFEDERATE VETERANS
GENERAL OFFICERS.
GEN. M. D. VANCE, Little Rock, Ark.................Commander in Chief
GEN. H. R. LEE, Nashville, Tenn........Adjutant General and Chief of Staff
MRS. W. B. KERNAN, 7219 Elm Street, New Orleans, La.
                                    Assistant to the Adjutant General
GEN. W. D. MATTHEWS, Oklahoma City, Okla.............Chaplain General

DEPARTMENT COMMANDERS.
GEN. E. D. TAYLOR, Richmond, Va..............Army of Northern Virginia
GEN. HAL T. WALKER, Montgomery, Ala.................Army of Tennessee
GEN. J. C. FOSTER, Houston, Tex.......................Trans-Mississippi

DIVISION COMMANDERS.
ALABAMA—Jasper...................................Gen. T. P. Lamkin
ARKANSAS—Little Rock...............................Gen. J. W. Hollis
FLORIDA—Tallahassee.............................Gen. T. J. Appleyard
GEORGIA—Vidalia.................................Gen. M. G. Murchison
KENTUCKY—Richmond............................Gen. N. B. Deatherage
LOUISIANA—Shreveport..............................Gen. H. C. Rogers
MARYLAND—Baltimore.............................Gen. H. M. Wharton
MISSISSIPPI—Magnolia..............................Gen. W. M. Wroten
MISSOURI—Kansas City............................Gen. A. A. Pearson
NORTH CAROLINA, Ansonville.........................Gen. W. A. Smith
OKLAHOMA—Tulsa..................................Gen. J. A. Yeager
SOUTH CAROLINA—Columbia.......................Gen. D. W. McLaurin
TENNESSEE—Nashville.............................Gen. John P. Hickman
TEXAS—Abilene....................................Gen. R. A. Miller
VIRGINIA—Petersburg............................Gen. Homer Atkinson
WEST VIRGINIA—Lewisburg.......................Gen. Thomas H. Dennis
CALIFORNIA—Los Angeles............................Gen. S. S. Simmons

HONORARY APPOINTMENTS.
GEN. C. I. WALKER, Charleston, S. C.........Honorary Commander for Life
GEN. JAMES A. THOMAS, Dublin, Ga............Honorary Commander for Life
GEN. K. M. VAN ZANDT, Fort Worth, Tex......Honorary Commander for Life
GEN. W. B. FREEMAN, Richmond, Va..........Honorary Commander for Life
REV. GILES B. COOKE, Mathews, Va......Honorary Chaplain General for Life

ADJUTANT GENERAL, ARMY OF TENNESSEE DEPARTMENT, U. C. V.

To fill the vacancy caused by the death of Gen. Hampden Osborne, Adjutant General, Army of Tennessee Department, U. C. V., on December 21, 1926, and that of Gen. W. A. Rawls, First Assistant Adjutant General, on December 6, 1926, Gen. Paul G. Sanguinetti, of Montgomery, Ala., has been appointed by Gen. Hal T. Walker, Commanding Army of Tennessee Department, U. C. V., to assume the duties of the office of the Adjutant General immediately.

U. C. V. INTERESTS.

An important resolution will come before the delegates to the thirty-seventh annual reunion, United Confederate Veterans, at Tampa, Fla., as an amendment to Article III, Section 2, providing for the filling of the unexpired term of the office of Commander in Chief, caused by death or resignation during his tenure of office. This amendment authorizes and empowers the three Lieutenant Generals of the organization, commanding the Departments of the Army of Northern Virginia, the Army of Tennessee, and the Trans-Mississippi, to select one of their number to assume and hold the office of Commander in Chief until the next annual reunion. This amendment is to be introduced for the purpose of avoiding any confusion incident to the possibility that none of the department commanders held commissions in the Confederate army, on which the succession has heretofore been made.

* * *

The one term rule for Commander in Chief will also be advocated at the Tampa reunion. This measure is favored by many prominent veterans, who feel that all should have a share in that honor now.

Enthusiastic friends of Gen. Edgar D. Taylor, of Richmond, Va., present Commander of the Army of Northern Virginia Department, will present his name before the convention at Tampa as the next Commander in Chief.

"The Tennessee Division Special" (L & N. R. R.), leaving Nashville for Tampa on Sunday, April 3, by way of Montgomery, Ala., will be entertained by the citizens and Daughters of the Confederacy of that city en route to Tampa and returning. At Jacksonville, Fla., breakfast will be served to the veterans of the party by the Daughters of the Confederacy, and lunch will be served at Orlando. Arrival at Tampa on Monday, April 4, 6:30 P.M. On the return trip, Daughters of the Confederacy and the civic societies of Montgomery jointly will entertain the veterans with lunch and a sightseeing trip on Saturday, April 9. Stop-overs have been arranged as follows: Jacksonville, one and a half hours; Orlando, one hour; Montgomery, three hours

Confederate Veteran.
Office: Methodist Publishing House Building, Nashville, Tenn.

E. D. POPE, EDITOR.

APOLOGIZING FOR THE SOUTH.

The favorite pursuit of some of the present-day intellectuals of the South, when invited to make addresses in the North or other sections of the country, seems to be the belittling of the South and her institutions, making comparison of her accomplishments with other sections, and especially in these years since the War between the States. It seems rather remarkable that this benighted South should be able to entertain or instruct an audience outside of the Mason and Dixon Line. One of these recently made a talk before the Southern Society of New York City, in which he followed the favorite trail, and thus gave evidence of ignorance and lack of appreciation of his native section. Matthew Page Andrews, Historian, "corrects the foolish and misleading assertions of Southern 'Educator'" in a letter to the *Baltimore Sun:*

"*To the Editor of the Sun—Sir:* Your dispatch from New York quotes Dr. Edwin Mims, professor of English at Vanderbilt University, as saying before the Southern Society:

"'There is a South that boasts of its original contribution to the nation in the organization of the Ku-Klux Klan, and there is a South that believes that the Klan is un-American and un-Christian.'

"Now one may scarcely conceive of an assertion which is more historically unsound and presently misleading. Dr. Mims talks of two wholly different things belonging to different periods as if they were one and the same thing!

"The Ku-Klux Klan, which rescued the South from the destructive forces of 'reconstruction' misrule, is not to be thought of as in any way connected with the recently organized society which has assumed the nomenclature of the erstwhile protector of political institutions. The old organization preserved for the good of the Federal republic what political scavengers had about to seize and destroy. The new organization appears to appeal chiefly to religious prejudices; and, in reaching for political power, it has expanded more successfully in the North than in the South.

"Is it possible that Dr. Mims does not know these facts? Or was he careless in his phraseology in an effort to turn a striking antithesis or some other figure of speech?

"Dr. Mims is correct in saying that Southerners (of the professional or blatant type) place an overemphasis upon 'the chivalry, manners, and hospitality' of the South—so much so, in fact, that one gets weary of hearing the terms; but when he calls upon Southerners to 'have done even with Southern ideals and traditions,' it is fitting to tell Dr. Mims that he has foolishly or thoughtlessly attempted to belittle the birthright of a common country, the invaluable heritage not only of the South, but of the nation.

"In all this he argues himself ignorant of historical fundamentals, which the good people of Boston and New York are as desirous of preserving as their compatriots in Richmond or New Orleans.

"Dr. Mims is sound enough in protesting against any shackling of reason and liberal thought in the departments of literature and the sciences. Historically, however, he has presented a distorted picture, and, lest any of those reading the aforesaid excerpts may have been misled, this explanation is presented by way of correction."

IN THE FAR WEST.

Daughters of the Confederacy in the far West have much to contend with of which those in their native section have no knowledge, and they are to be commended for their perseverance in the work. For instance, Mrs. A. W. Ollor, of Tacoma, Wash., wanted to present pictures of some of our Southern heroes to the schools of that city, and in an interview with the Superintendent of Schools, after he had conferred with the principals, he stated that he thought it unwise at this time to put them in, "that the youth of the land had been taught that Jefferson Davis was an arch traitor," etc., Mrs. Ollor told him that the whole world had recognized R. E. Lee as a great American and "*they*" would have to learn that Jefferson Davis was a Christian gentleman and patriot—and she would not place any of the portraits unless Jefferson Davis was included. She finally obtained permission to place the portraits in the different schools if there was to be no ceremony nor display or anything in the papers. "If you think that the war is over," Mrs. Ollor writes, "come to Tacoma, and I'll prove to you that it isn't."

COMMENDS THE VETERAN.

In renewing his subscription for another year, George D. Ewing, of Pattonsburg, Mo., improves the occasion by writing:

"I became a subscriber to the VETERAN only four years after it was established by the late S. A. Cunningham, whose great aim was to make it the medium for authentic history of the South. It was a success from the beginning.

"While most of the original contributors, who wrote of stirring events which they had personally witnessed, have gone to their reward, the duty of continuing this important historial publication has been largely transmitted to a younger generation.... May the descendants of the brave, historic South prove equal to the important task of preserving the history of those epochal times in book form for the now living as well as those who may come after them. This history is aglow with courage and honor, which is not exceeded in any period in the world's chronicled events. This history as it actually occurred has been gathered and collated more particularly by Confederate veterans. Why should not succeeding generations of our Southland take much interest, as well as much pride, in preserving and perpetuating the history of their forbears? It so clearly shows the indomitable courage of a noble people from whom they sprang. Maintain and extend the circulation of the VETERAN, for by this knowledge of the past you may be justly proud of your ancestry."

SONNET TO THE CONFEDERATE DEAD.
BY W. H. GIBBS, COLUMBIA, S. C.

The thought of war is surging on the mind,
And of the heroes that for country bled,
When hostile hordes o'er that loved country spread;
Of how they left all selfishness behind,
And deemed the fate that thus destroyed them kind
If battle's tide were stemmed by blood they shed,
Or back they turned invading army's tread.
With noble courage, unto danger blind,
How gloriously they fought and grandly fell!
And yet, tho' fallen, they seem victors still,
Since deathless history their deeds shall tell,
And gratitude to them our hearts shall fill,
And through the ages peal memorial bell,
And they, tho' dead, shall yet the living thrill.

SAM DAVIS.

The world was beautiful. Of it he dreamed;
  Its misty highways waited, leading far
To where, above their golden limits, gleamed
  Life's twilight star.

Under the guardian hills so dear to him,
  Held in the green heart of his native State,
Stood the old homestead, and, eyes grown dim,
  Within its gate

Watched the sweet, hopeful mother, with her trusting face
  Seeking the lifted hills whence help must come,
Praying as only Southern mothers could,
  "Lord, bring him home!"

But yonder stretched high honor's narrow way,
  By less discerning eyes yet undescried.
Though the black shadow of a gallows lay
  Across this side,

He faltered not. Lo, how the star he'd dreamed
  Would shine upon him in life's twilight space
Burst from the beauty of the morning skies and leaned
  To kiss his face!

Lo, how the glory he had thought would shine
  From sundown skies upon his evening way
Robed him in splendor as he passed at morn
  Proud honor's way!   —*Beatrice Stevens.*

AT THE GRAVE OF SAM DAVIS.

SAM DAVIS MEMORIAL PARK.

More than sixty years ago a tragedy was enacted at Pulaski, Tenn., by which a young soldier of the Confederacy gave up his life rather than betray the confidence which had been reposed in him. For over thirty years he lay in the quiet grave in the garden of his old home at Smyrna, Tenn., near Murfreesboro, a place made beautiful by a father's tender care, but his sacrifice unknown save by those who had known him in life—a narrow circle for even the greatest, and he was only of that great middle class which does not seek publicity. Over thirty years he had rested there when it was given to the late Dr. J. M. King, then a student at Peabody College in Nashville and whose father had been a fellow soldier of the young hero, to write the wonderful story of Sam Davis, of Tennessee, and this was read before his class. Later he brought it to the editor of the VETERAN, and it was published in the number for May, 1894, and thus was first given to the world the story of the boy soldier whose heroism has not a parallel in history.

The publication of this story brought from others further accounts of the boy soldier's service and sacrifice, not only from those who had served with him, but from those who had fought against him, and out of it all grew the determination to erect to him a monument that would keep his memory green. Sponsored by the late S. A. Cunningham, founder and editor of the VETERAN, a fund was collected and a handsome monument erected on Capitol Hill in Nashville. There is also a monument to him in Pulaski, on the spot where he was executed. Now another movement is under way to have the old home place preserved as a memorial museum and park as a tribute by the State of Tennessee to a son whose life and death have shed luster upon the commonwealth. It will be most fitting indeed to so dedicate the birthplace and boyhood home of Sam Davis and thus keep before the present and future generations of Tennesseeans an example of patriotic self-sacrifice that will be an inspiration to other sons to develop that high character which is the bulwark of a State.

This movement is being sponsored by Dr. J. S. Lowry, of Smyrna, Tenn., who will be glad to give information about it, and he will shortly announce the committees by which the work will be carried on. Friends can help by writing to members of the legislature to support this movement when it comes before them.

Over his beloved boy the heartbroken father erected a handsome monument, and in its shadow the parents, too, were laid when called from earth. On that monument is inscribed:

"In Memory of Samuel Davis,
A member of the 1st Tennessee Regiment of Volunteers.
Born October 6, 1842; died November 27, 1863,
Aged 21 years, 1 month, and 21 days.
He laid down his life for his country.
A Truer Soldier, a Purer Patriot, a Braver Man
Never Lived. He suffered death on the gibbet
Rather than betray his friends and country."

Capt. J. W. Mathews, of Alvon, W. Va., one of the survivors of the "Immortal Six hundred," and now in his eighty-eighth year, renews his subscription for two years more. He was in the war from start to finish, except when in prison. He commanded Company I, 25th Virginia Infantry. He is anxious to get a copy of the book on "The Immortal Six Hundred," and will appreciate hearing from anyone who has this book for sale.

GENERAL LEE'S LETTER TO LORD ACTON.

This letter, written while General Lee was President of Washington College, is unique, since its author was extremely cautious and reticent among his own people on the subject which he here discussed freely with his foreign correspondent. It will be found in Lord Acton's "Correspondence," Volume I. This letter should be annually recalled on January 19 and read as a part of the exercises in commemoration of that anniversary:

"LEXINGTON, VA., December 15, 1866.

"*Sir:* Although your letter of the 4th ulto. has been before me some days unanswered, I hope you will not attribute it to a want of interest in the subject, but to my inability to keep pace with my correspondence. As a citizen of the South, I feel deeply indebted to you for the sympathy you have evinced in its cause and am conscious that I owe your kind consideration of myself to my connection with it. The influence of current opinion in Europe upon the current politics of America must always be salutary, and the importance of the questions now at issue in the United States, involving not only constitutional government in this country, but the progress of universal liberty and civilization, invests your proposition with peculiar value and will add to the obligation which every true American must owe you for your efforts to guide that opinion aright. Amid the conflicting statements and sentiments in both countries, it will be no easy task to discover the truth or to relieve it from the mass of prejudice and passion with which it has been covered by party spirit. I am conscious of the compliment conveyed in your request for my opinion as to the light in which American politics should be viewed, and, had I the ability, I have not the time to enter upon a discussion which was commenced by the founders of the Constitution and has been continued to the present day. I can only say that while I have considered the preservation of the constitutional power of the general government to be the foundation of our peace and safety at home and abroad, I yet believe that the maintenance of the rights and authority reserved to the States and to the people not only essential to the adjustment and balance of the general system, but the safeguard to the continuance of a free government. I consider it as the chief source of stability to our political system, whereas the consolidation of the States into one vast republic, sure to be aggressive abroad and despotic at home, will be the certain precursor of that ruin which has overwhelmed all those that have preceded it. I need not refer one so well acquainted as you are with American history to the state papers of Washington and Jefferson, the representatives of the federal and democratic parties, denouncing consolidation and centralization of power as tending to the subversion of State governments and to despotism. The New England States, whose citizens are the fiercest opponents of the Southern States, did not always avow the opinions they now advocate. Upon the purchase of Louisiana by Jefferson, they virtually asserted the right of secession through their prominent men; and in the convention which assembled at Hartford in 1814, they threatened the disruption of the Union unless the war should be discontinued. The assertion of this right has been repeatedly made by their politicians when their party was weak, and Massachusetts, the leading State in hostility to the South, declares in the preamble of her constitution that the people of that commonwealth 'have the sole and exclusive right of government themselves as a free, sovereign, and independent State, and do, and forever hereafter shall,exercise and enjoy every power, jurisdiction, and right which is not or may hereafter be by them expressly delegated to the United States of America in congress assembled.' Such has been in substance the language of every other State government and such doctrine advocated by the leading men of the country for the last seventy years. Judge Chase, the present Chief Justice of the United States, as late as 1850, is reported to have stated in the Senate, of which he was a member, that he 'knew of no remedy in case of the refusal of a State to perform its stipulations,' thereby acknowledging the sovereignty and independence of State action.

"But I will not weary you with this unprofitable discussion, unprofitable because the judgment of reason has been displaced by the arbitrament of war, waged for the purpose, as avowed, of maintaining the union of the States. If, therefore, the result of the war is to be considered as having decided that the union of the States is inviolable and perpetual under the Constitution, it naturally follows that it is as incompetent for the general government to impair its integrity by the exclusion of a State as for the States to do so by secession, and that the existence and rights of a State by the Constitution are as indestructible as the Union itself. The legitimate consequence then must be the perfect equality of rights of all the States, the exclusive right of each to regulate its internal affairs under rules established by the Constitution, and the right of each State to prescribe for itself the qualifications of suffrage. The South has contended only for the supremacy of the Constitution and the just administration of the laws made in pursuance of it. Virginia to the last made great efforts to save the Union and urged harmony and compromise. Senator Douglas, in his remarks upon the compromise bill recommended by the committee of thirteen in 1861, stated that every member from the South, including Messrs, Toombs and Davis, expressed their willingness to accept the proposition of Senator Crittenden, of Kentucky, as a final settlement of the controversy if sustained by the Republican party, and that the only difficulty in the way of an amicable adjustment was with the Republican party. Who, then, is responsible for the war? Although the South would have preferred any honorable compromise to the fratricidal war which has taken place, she now accepts in good faith its constitutional results, and receives without reserve the amendment which has already been made to the Constitution for the extinction of slavery. That is an event that has been long sought, though in a different way, and by none has it been more earnestly desired than by the citizens of Virginia. In other respects I trust that the Constitution may undergo no change, but that it may be handed down to succeeding generations in the form we received it from our forefathers.

"The desire I feel that the Southern States should possess the good opinion of one whom I esteem as highly as yourself has caused me to extend my remarks farther than I intended, and I fear it has led me to exhaust your patience. If what I have said should serve to give any information as regards American politics, and enable you to enlighten public opinion as to the true interests of this distracted country, I hope you will pardon its prolixity.

"In regard to your inquiry as to my being engaged in preparing a narrative of the campaigns in Virginia, I regret to state that I progress slowly in the collection of the necessary documents for its completion. I particularly feel the loss of the official returns showing the small numbers with which the battles were fought. I have not seen the work of the Prussian officer you mention and, therefore, cannot speak of his accuracy in this respect.

"With sentiments of great respect, I remain,
"Your obedient servant, R. E. LEE."

ABOLITION—NORTHERN AND SOUTHERN VIEWS AND PLANS.

BY MRS. TEXA BOWEN WILLIAMS, HISTORIAN MARY CUSTIS LEE CHAPTER, U. D. C., LOS ANGELES, CALIF.

(This essay won the Rose Loving Cup, Richmond Convention, U. D. C., 1926.)

From the early colonial period, the germs of the abolition movement lived in the North and the South perhaps with equal virility. The seed had two issues, the political and the moral.

Every one of the thirteen colonies at some time held slaves. The Constitution gave the right, and they saw no harm in it. But the slave trade itself soon became a source of grave concern, and the Southern States really seemed more concerned than the Northern. Massachusetts was the first State to legislate in favor of slavery, and Georgia the first to legislate against it. It was this traffic in slavery and the inhuman methods used in capturing and shipping these negroes from Africa which first aroused sentiment against slavery. The slave trade was begun and carried on principally by Massachusetts, not privately, but by authority of the Plymouth Colony (Colonial Entry Book, V, 4, p. 724). This business was continued because it was found to be profitable. Faneuil Hall, the "Cradle of Liberty," was built with money Peter Faneuil made in slave traffic. (Rutherford: The Civilization of the Old South.) Many times during colonial days the South legislated against slavery, the Virginia House of Burgesses passing twenty-three acts prohibiting the further importation of slaves; but the king vetoed them all, so profitable had the traffic become to England. Georgia forbade slavery when the colony was founded, but after fourteen years its policy was reversed and laws were passed introducing slave labor. Whether this was due to change of heart through economic need or reversal of moral sentiment wholly, who can say?

Thomas Jefferson was author of the first bill to allow a slaveholder to free his slaves. At his instigation a committee of five Virginians was appointed to revise the laws and prepare all slaveholders in the State for gradual emancipation of their slaves. Thirty-two times Virginia legislated against slavery. George Washington freed his slaves in his will. George Mason, John Randolph, Henry Clay, Robert E. Lee, and hundreds of others freed their slaves at their own economic loss. They advocated gradual emancipation. Before 1820, there had been hundreds of thousands of negroes freed in the South. In 1826, there were in the United States one hundred and forty-three abolition societies, one hundred and three of which were in the South. This one hundred and three comprised five-sixths of the total membership. Be it remembered these men were not trying to free some one else's slaves, but their own property, bought with their own money. The North during this time had also been emancipating its slaves, though in a different manner. Emancipation began in Vermont in 1777. It gradually spread over the other States, "from no conscientious scruples, but simply because the slave labor was unprofitable" (Fisk's Critical Period, p. 73). The North never freed her slaves; she sold them to Southern markets (Ingram: History of Slavery, p. 184, London). So long as the North owned slaves, their consciences slept; but where was the New England slave trade, infinitely more brutal and inhuman than any phase of slavery ever was, was in progress? In the beginning, condemnation of slavery was predicated on gentle and holy morals, but after the unnatural alliance of hate, obloquy, and religion, the movement changed rapidly into an inveterate crusade against slavery, led by the Abolition Party. William Lloyd Garrison began publishing his *Liberator* in January, 1831. Denunciation and epithet were his weapons. His methods were radical—I. W. W. put to shame. He declared in the first issue for immediate enfranchisement of all slaves: "I do not wish to think, or speak, or write with moderation" —and he never did. Seven months after the first copy of the *Liberator* was issued, Nat Turner's insurrection took place, resulting in the massacre of sixty-one white men, women, and children. Nat Turner could read and had been known to have read some of Garrison's incendiary pamphlets sent out from Boston (Hart: Slavery and Abolition). Garrison was denounced by the sane and thinking of the North. He could not hire a hall, and his printing press was finally demolished by a street mob in Boston.

The best people, North and South, favored the antislavery movement as it proceeded, 1770 to 1831, in a natural and orderly manner. But by 1838, the *Liberator, Emancipator, Philanthropist, National Enquirer,* and *New York Evangelist* were reaching the homes of thousands in the North. This issue, involving a moral question, as is always the case, bred bigoted radicals who, through temperament, made everything personal and became combative and abusive toward whoever challenged the wisdom of their views. In 1854, Framington, Mass., the Abolitionists celebrated the Fourth of July thus: William Lloyd Garrison held to public gaze and burned before a multitude, copies of

1. The Fugitive Slave Law.
2. Several legal decisions in favor of the South.
3. Then he held up the Constitution of the United States, saying it was the "parent of all other atrocities, a covenant with death and an agreement with hell," consumed it to ashes, exclaiming: "So perish all compromises with tyranny."

The methods of these radicals bore little of political practicability, social justice, or reason. Only for the effect of their blundering do they deserve discussion, for when an effort is made to determine fundamental valuations, men of fixed convictions are not worth consulting. Such men do not see below themselves, for convictions are prisons. To know the truth, go to an open-minded man, not to one who would persecute for the sake of an idea. Some sort of persecution is all that is needed at any time to give an honorable name to the most indifferent doctrine. So, as the contention grew, the South tightened her hold on her rights and reversed much of her leniency of opinion. Garrison was dragged through the streets of Boston, and this persecution made many friends for his cause. Garrison and his assistants possessed the spirit of martyrs, but they never proved the truth of their cause. No martyrs ever did, for they seldom have anything to do with the truth. In this case "all their actions tended to incendiarism and anarchy. Garrison was a bomb thrower, and he declared the Southern planter a 'criminal, oppressor, and pirate.'" (Schouler: History of United States, p. 214). They, however, enlisted sympathy and solicited money from men in the North to import Abolition speakers (A. B. Hart: Slavery and Abolition, p. 214). William E. Channing and others declared there was a higher law than the Constitution. Channing wrote his histories as "pot boilers," said Dr. Adams, and Dr. Adams is one of America's greatest historians to-day. Many others have written in this same way about the War between the States. The slave problem in the South was so colored by other issues, it is difficult to write without mentioning some of them. All reform is slow, working like a leaven, until the time is ripe for action. The great problem in the minds of all conservatives was what to do with the negroes when freed. Lincoln said: "If all earthly power were given me, I should not know what to do as to the existing institution. We cannot free them and make them our equals. A system of gradual emancipation might be adopted, and I will not undertake to judge our Southern friends too harshly in this matter." When John Randolph freed his negroes, he bought territory in Ohio and placed them on it. To-day that territory contains the city of Zanesville, the seat of a large college for negroes. Jefferson Davis urged in the United States Senate that some plan be devised for freeing the negroes, some plan that would be fair to both the slave and to the master. President Monroe and some associates in Congress colonized some slaves in Africa, in the richest district they could find. As soon as these colonists were left alone, their failure at self-government was complete.

The agitators, in spite of social ostracism and political disapproval, continued their crusade. They imported intemperate lecturers. George Thompson, one of these, on an inflammatory tour, said in a speech that Southern slaves ought, or, at least had a right, to cut the throats of their masters. But even Boston became too hot for him, and after being threatened with tar and feathers and lynching he left for a healthier climate and he left secretly (Schouler: History of the United States, pp. 217–18). But the earnestness of these people and the abstract rightness of their cause finally won for them many friends. The Nat Turner insurrection, the Southampton Massacre—mostly women and children—and the John Brown raid alarmed the South to the highest pitch, and no wonder. These murders were condoned by the Northern government and excused in the name of "liberty." Daniel Webster disliked slavery, but his conciliation speech, his great "seventh of March speech," caused the alienation of most of his friends. He said: "I am against agitators, North and South, and all narrow, local contests. I am an American, and I know no locality but America." His speech infuriated Seward, Sumner, and their followers. Horace Mann said: "Webster is a fallen star." Sumner declared: "Webster has placed himself in the dark list of apostates." The poet Whittier sang in apt verse:

"Let not the land once proud of him
Mourn for him now,
Nor brand with deeper shame his dim
Dishonored brow.

Then pay the reverence of old days
To his dead fame!
Walk backward with averted gaze
And hide his shame."

All this because he refused to support insurrection and tyranny!

The South was further concerned by the passage of the "Personal Liberty Laws" in contradiction to the Federal Fugitive Slave Law. Mr. Webster said that under the Constitution the South had the right to ask the repeal of these laws. This adherence to existing law was one of the points upon which the North turned against Webster, who thus destroyed for himself the probability of becoming President, the goal of his life's ambition. The South looked upon the Constitution as the Puritan did his Bible. Jefferson had included a clause prohibiting slavery when he framed the Constitution, but it displeased John Adams, of Massachusetts, so it was omitted. The Southerners believed that willing submission to law is one of the highest qualities of national character, and its evasion impaired the moral character of its people (The Old South: Thomas Nelson Page), and that from opposition to law to lawlessness itself is but a step; and so it proved. The harvest must be of the nature of the seed that are sown.

From 1830 to 1860, no more active cause of strife existed than the writings of the Abolitionists. All sorts of methods of distribution were resorted to. The South was deluged with incendiary pamphlets whose tendency was to incite the slaves to rise against their masters. The South had already received a bitter taste of this in the Southampton Massacre and others (Schouler: p. 216). Tracts and periodicals printed for this purpose with pictures even more inflammatory than the texts they illustrated were struck off by the thousands, some printed on cheap muslin handkerchiefs, and deposited in the mails of the South. A package of these discovered in the mails at Philadelphia was taken to the middle of the Delaware River and sunk. In Charleston the mail pouches were emptied, and three thousand citizens watched the bonfire at night made by this "literature." The Postmaster General justified this in two ways, the extremity of the situation, and he ruled that the United States ought not to trasmit matter which State laws had prohibited, thus upholding a principle of State Rights. So the local postmasters threw out this seditious matter and were not punished for it.

"Old John Brown," as the Southerners called him, was not a product of this propaganda, but one of the propagators of all the trouble. Surely those who try to canonize him would have a hard time to find any saintly qualities if they look honestly into his life history. Dr. Hodder (University of Kansas) says if he had not been hanged he would have gone down in history as a common horse thief. He might, too, have said "murderer." The truth is, he murdered the Doyle family that night to cover the theft of their horses. Horse stealing in Missouri and Kansas in that day was a criminal offense, usually punished by mob or hanging. Murder was no serious matter. He knew he was safe because the Doyles were Southern sympathizers. Brown's death at Harper's Ferry received scant sympathy from the Southern people. A bit of doggerel illustrates the optimism and derision which would crop up in the gravest time:

"At Harper's Ferry Section, there was an insurrection,
John Brown thought the niggers would sustain him;
But old Governor Wise put his specs upon his eyes
And drove him from the happy land of Canaan."

Burgess says: "Nothing could have been more wickedly harmful and positively diabolical than the John Brown raid. If the whole thing both as to time, methods, and results, had been planned by his Satanic Majesty himself it could not have succeeded better in setting the sound conservative movements of the age at naught. It cannot be regarded other than one of the chiefest crimes in history." (Burgess: The Civil War and the Constitution.)

We have never believed in Sumner's "Irrepressible Conflict." Time has proved the South right in all her contentions, but the war proved nothing. Disraeli spoke truly: "War is never a solution; it is an aggravation." David Starr Jordan said: "Wars are brought on by human blundering," and "It is an affront to Divinity itself to assert that the world's civilization cannot be realized except through violence and destruction, blood, crime, and sin."

ERROR.—A mistake was made in crediting Col. D. W. Timberlake with the authorship of the poem on "Old Trees," published in the VETERAN for April, 1926, page 133. The poem is one of Father Ryan's, and Colonel Timberlake sent a copy of it to the VETERAN, and his name was used with it by mistake.

ARMORIES OF THE CONFEDERACY.

BY RICHARD D. STEUART, BALTIMORE, MD.

In previous articles in the VETERAN, I have tried to tell something about the hand weapons—guns, swords, pistols—used by Confederate soldiers. This article aims to list briefly the armories, government and State, and the private manufactories which furnished small arms for the Confederate armies. If anyone can augment this list or furnish additional information about those listed, the data will be welcome.

The outbreak of the war found the South without any armory or machinery for the manufacture of firearms, except the Federal armory at Harper's Ferry, which was burned by the United States troops guarding it, and small obsolete plants at Columbia, S. C., Fayetteville, N. C., and Richmond, Va. From the Harper's Ferry ruins, however, the Confederate authorities saved a lot of material and machinery for making the rifle and rifle musket. This was the nucleus of its arms-making enterprises.

On September 30, 1863, General Gorgas, Chief of Ordnance, reported to the Secretary of War that Richmond, Fayetteville, and Asheville, N. C., had produced 28,000 small arms and private factories about 7,000 more. On December 31, 1864, he reported that government armories were in operation at Richmond, Fayetteville, Columbia, S. C., Athens, Ga., and Tallassee, Ala.

Thus we are shown at this date only a few months before the collapse of the Confederacy, five government armories, as follows:

Richmond.—Machinery for making the 1855 model rifle musket was removed from Harper's Ferry and set up in the State Armory at Richmond, which had been in existence since the early part of the nineteenth century. Operations for the Confederacy were started in September, 1861, and the output reached as high as 1,000 guns a month.

Fayetteville, N. C.—Machinery for making the 1855 rifle was removed from Harper's Ferry and set up in the old Arsenal. Operations were begun in the spring of 1862, and the output reached as high as 400 a month.

Columbia, S. C.—General Gorgas reported in December, 1864, that the output of the Columbia Armory could be increased to 4,000 a month. In all probability this was the old Palmetto Armory, which in the early fifties turned out muskets, rifles, and pistols for the State. It was operated at that time by William Glaze & Co.

Athens, Ga.—The plant of Cook & Brother was established in New Orleans at the outbreak of the war and made excellent rifles and carbines on the Enfield model. When New Orleans was captured, the machinery for making arms was carried on flatboats to Athens, where it was installed in modern brick buildings. The output at Athens was as high as 300 guns a day, it is reported, although the figure seems exaggerated.

Tallassee, Ala.—This plant for the manufacture of muzzle-loading carbines was removed from Richmond in 1863. It was expected to turn out 150 carbines a day. Prior to 1863, breech-loading carbines were made at Tallassee on a small scale by private parties.

In addition to these government armories, there were many State and private arms plants, including the following:

W. S. McElwaine, also known as Jones, McElwaine & Co., Holly Springs, Miss. This firm was given the first government contract for 30,000 rifles. It was set up in the old foundry of the Marshall County Manufacturing Company and turned out guns at the rate of twenty-five a day until the advance of the enemy compelled removal of the machinery, probably to Macon, Ga.

Arkadelphia, Ark.—Rifles were made there early in the war. The machinery was removed to Marshall, Tex.

Little Rock, Ark.—Gun-making machinery owned by the State removed to Tyler, Tex.

Tyler, Tex.—Tyler was the ordnance headquarters for the Trans-Mississippi Department. Yarborough, Short & Briscoe started the manufacture of rifles. Their plant was taken over by the government, and the machinery, with that removed from Little Rock, Ark., was used for the manufacture of rifles on the Enfield model.

Marshall, Tex.—Plant built up from machinery removed from Arkadelphia, Ark.

Bonham, Tex.—Rifles officially reported to have been made there.

Tucker, Sherrod & Co., Lancaster, Tex.—This firm was awarded a contract to make Colt model revolvers. The contract was cancelled after a few had been made in both army and navy sizes.

Whitescarver, Campbell & Co., Rusk, Tex.—Awarded contract to make 900 rifles.

Billings & Hassell, Plenitude, Tex.—Awarded contract to make 1,200 rifles.

N. O. Tanner, Bastrop, Tex.—Given rifle contract.

Nashville, Tenn.—Rifles were made here, but by whom it is not known.

Pulaski, Tenn.—Rifles made there.

Memphis Arms Company, Memphis, Tenn.—Incorporated in 1861, but did not operate.

Gallatin, Tenn.—Rifles reported made there.

S. C. Robinson Arms Manufactory, Richmond, Va.—This firm made carbines on the Sharp's model. The government took over the plant, it becoming the C. S. Carbine Works, and converted it into a factory for the manufacture of muzzle-loading carbines. The plant was removed to Tallassee, Ala.

Union Manufacturing Company, Richmond, Va.—Also known as J. P. Sloat's Rifle Factory. It began to make guns early in 1861 and employed two hundred hands. Nothing is known of the kind or quantity of its output.

Samuel Sutherland, Richmond, Va.—Sutherland had a large plant for remaking, remodeling, and converting firearms. It is doubtful if he made any weapons originally in 1861-65.

Robinson & Lester, Richmond, Va.—They made revolvers on the Whitney model.

Thomas W. Cofer, Portsmouth, Va.—Invented a revolver and manufactured it on a small scale.

J. B. Barrett, Wytheville, Va.—He assembled guns from parts saved from the ruins of the Harper's Ferry armory at the rate of eight or ten a day in 1861, and also made new guns.

Danville, Va.—Carbines made there at a factory, the owner of which is unknown.

Huntersville, Va.—The records refer to a Sharp's carbine factory there.

Mendenhall, James & Gardner, Greensboro, N. C.—This firm had a contract to make rifles for the State of North Carolina.

Lamb & Brother, Jamestown, N. C.—This firm was given a contract for 10,000 rifles for the State. The output was 300 a month.

Pullem, Asheville, N. C.—A small factory for the manufacture of rifles was started by Pullem at Asheville. The plant was taken over by the government, and later the machinery was removed to Columbia, S. C.

Garrett Brothers, Greensboro, N. C.—They are said to have made rifles and pistols.

Edward Want, New Bern, N. C.—He obtained a contract to make pistols for the government, but it is not believed any were made.

J. H. Tarpley, Greensboro, N. C.—Tarpley invented a breech-loading carbine and manufactured it on a small scale.

George W. Morse, Greenville, S. C.—Morse, who was an inventor of many improvements for firearms, was superintendent of the Nashville Arsenal in 1861. He set up a plant at Greenville, known as the State Works. There he made breech-loading carbines of his own model and muzzle loading muskets with his own patented lock. The plant was closed and sold at auction in November, 1864.

Alabama Arms Manufacturing Company, Montgomery, Ala.—Officially reported to have made excellent Enfield model rifles.

Winters Iron Works, Montgomery, Ala.—Made rifles.

Montgomery Arsenal, Ala.

Talladega, Ala.—There was a small arms plant there, which was destroyed by Federal raiders in August, 1864. Probably Sturdivant's factory making Mississippi Rifles.

J. F. Dittrick, Mobile, Ala.—He was a well-known gunsmith before the war and is believed to have made guns for the Confederacy.

Dickson, Nelson & Co., Ala.—This firm was incorporated as the Shakanoosa Arms Manufacturing Company. It made rifles for the State of Alabama. The plant was erected at Dickson, Ala., then removed to Rome, Ga., where it was burned. It was moved again to Adairsville, Ga., and, after the battle of Chickamauga, to Dawson, Ga., where it was operated until the end of the war. It made Mississippi model rifles.

Selma, Ala.—Selma was a center of munitions operations, and it is said that a small arms factory at that place employed 3,000 hands.

Georgia Armory, Milledgeville, Ga.—This factory was established in the penitentiary by Gov. Joseph E. Brown in 1862, and was burned by Wilson's raiders in 1865. It turned out 125 guns a month. The records say they were muskets, but it is known that rifles marked "Georgia Armory" were made.

D. C. Hodgkins & Son, Macon, Ga.—This firm made rifles, the output being about 100 a month.

Macon, Ga.—The records refer to a government armory at that place.

Spiller & Burr, Macon and Atlanta, Ga.—They made revolvers on the Whitney model.

Leech & Rigdon, Augusta, Ga.—Made revolvers on the Colt model.

Greer's Pistol Factory, Griswoldville, Ga.—This factory was destroyed by Federal raiders in the campaign against Savannah.

Haiman & Brothers Pistol Factory, Columbus, Ga.—There are frequent references to this plant. Part of the machinery was removed to Tallassee, Ala., late in the war.

W. D. Bowen, Augusta, Ga.—Mentioned as a manufacturer of guns.

C. Chapman.—He manufactured Mississippi model rifles, but the site of his plant is not known.

Read's Factory.—There are frequent references in the record to Read's cavalry rifles, but nothing to show where or by whom they were made.

Tilton, Ga.—There was a musket factory there, but little is known of it.

"B. & B."—Rifles were made for the State of Alabama and stamped "B & B," but it is not known who the makers were or where they were located.

Brandon, Miss.—The Mississippi State Arsenal at Panola was removed to Brandon, still later to Meridian, and there is reason to believe that a few guns were made there.

Columbus, Ga.—Rifles and carbines were made here by the following:

J. P. Murray.—He made rifles and carbines.

Louis Haiman & Brother.—Made Mississippi model rifles.

Greenwood & Gray (believed to have been the same as J. P. Murray).

Columbus Iron Works.—Mississippi model rifles made there.

In the hands of collectors of firearms are many guns and pistols of unmistakably Confederate origin, but where or by whom they were made are mysteries. These weapons of unidentified origin include revolvers made on the Colt's model, breech-loading carbines, and a very curious conversion of the old Hall's breech-loading rifle to a muzzle loader.

FORREST'S WONDERFUL ACHIEVEMENTS.

CAPT. JAMES DINKINS, OF NEW ORLEANS.

After the battle of Chickamauga, Forrest tendered to General Bragg his resignation as brigadier general. He felt so depressed on account of the delay and the inaction in following up a great victory, and, furthermore, was dissatisfied with various conditions which seemed to indicate that he was not appreciated by the commander in chief.

For some time previously, Forrest had received urgent requests from prominent people in North Mississippi to come to that section and organize the scattered bands and defend their country from the frequent raids by the Federal forces at Memphis and along the Memphis and Charleston Railroad. That may also have had its influence upon Forrest's decision.

It happened that Mr. David was at General Bragg's headquarters when Forrest's resignation reached him, and he at once wrote Forrest in graceful language, saying he could not accept his resignation nor dispense with his services, and requested that he meet him at Montgomery a few days later. At the time designated, Forrest met the President, who promised to give him an independent command in the department of West Tennessee and North Mississippi, and also stated that Forrest should carry with him such regiments as General Bragg could spare.

However, when Forrest took his departure, he did so with McDonald's Battalion and Morton's Battery, besides his escort company, all told three hundred men and four guns. He reached the Mobile and Ohio Railroad at Okolona, Miss. on the 15th of November, 1863. He decided soon afterwards to move into West Tennessee and use his influence and prestige in bringing together numbers of men who had been furloughed on account of wounds and other causes and having recovered were not willing to go back to the infantry service. He, therefore, crossed the Memphis and Charleston Railroad at Saulsbury and moved to Jackson with 250 men and two rifle guns of Morton's battery. He reached Jackson on the 6th of December, 1863, and went into camp with as much composure and confidence as if he had a division instead of a few squadrons.

Major General Hurlbut, commanding the Federal forces at Memphis and West Tennessee also, set to work at once, to prevent Forrest's escape. He sent a force from Memphis, one from Corinth, and one from Fort Pillow, in all, about 20,000 men, well equipped, to accomplish that object.

Think of it! Forrest with but those five hundred men surrounded by twenty thousand veteran troops. No other man on earth so situated could have marched away. Forrest soon had assembled about three thousand men, who, however, had no arms, and to protect those men from capture with the aid of only three hundred men seemed impossible—but that word was not in Forrest's vocabulary.

About this time it began to rain and bad weather lasted several days, causing all the rivers and creeks to overflow their banks; but on December 22, Forrest put his column in motion, and crossed the Forked Deer River, going in the direction of Bolivar. His scouts reported large Federal forces moving on him from all sides, but, with about five hundred armed men and three thousand men without guns, he set out to reach the Confederate lines. Arriving at Bolivar, he was met by Col. D. M. Wisdom with one hundred and fifty men, which made his fighting force nearly seven hundred strong.

Ascertaining that a Federal column was encamped just south of the Hatchie River, and directly in the line of his intended march, Forrest constructed a bridge over the river during the night, and crossed over, and while the enemy were wrapped in slumber just before day, he dashed into their camp, creating the wildest confusion, and stampeded the entire force, which left behind a large number of wagons and several hundred head of beef cattle.

Forrest then moved rapidly in the direction of Somerville, where he learned that the whole country was swarming with infantry, cavalry, and artillery, ready to pounce on him. Forrest, with the additional responsibility of protecting his captured beef cattle and wagons, was in a hopeless position it would seem. Halting a few hours before reaching Somerville, he sent some three hundred armed men and about a thousand without arms to get in the Federal rear, and, moving boldly with the remainder of his command until he met the enemy's pickets, he drove them in. About the same time the detached force charged into the Federals on the other side, Forrest sent forward a flag of truce demanding the unconditional surrender of the enemy, consisting of 5,000 infantry and 2,000 cavalry, and the Federal commander, believing that he was surrounded by a large force, began a hurried retreat in the direction of Memphis. Taking advantage of the fright, Forrest led his escort company and McDonald's Battalion upon their retreating columns, riding them down and scattering them in all directions.

The victory was so complete that the unarmed men joined in the pursuit and captured several hundred prisoners, from whom they secured arms, etc.

Leaving the Federal command scattered and in great disorder, Forrest marched toward Memphis, creating the impression that he would attack the place, which caused the Federal commander, General Hurlbut, to hurry all the troops along the Memphis and Charleston Railroad, from Corinth westward to Memphis, and also recalled the forces he had sent from Fort Pillow. The heavy rains had in the meantime caused the Forked Deer, the Hatchie, and the Wolf rivers to overflow their banks, so that they could not be crossed at all, which left the Federal forces in Forrests rear utterly harmless.

While the enemy was hurrying to Memphis, Forrest suddenly changed his course to the south, and crossed the Memphis and Charleston Railroad at Mount Pleasant into the Confederate lines, with a thousand head of cattle and a large number of wagons and stores of different sorts. The cattle were sent to feed the Army of Tennessee.

Many amusing incidents occurred during the stampede of the Federal forces at Somerville. In the pursuit of a column of these fugitives, a Confederate officer, Lieutenant Livingston, received orders to turn back with his company. He shouted after them: "Get out of our country, you worthless rascals."

In the rear of the Federals, on a horse somewhat slower than the rest, was a trooper, who, turning his head, exclaimed in unmistakable brogue and with the ready wit of his countrymen: "Faith, ain't it thot same we're trying to do jist as fast as we can?"

Forrest had then reached safe ground, and we can but wonder how it was possible for him to escape with his wagons, cattle, and unarmed men in the face of the manifold dangers which environed him.

Leaving Jackson, Tenn., on a march of one hundred and fifty miles, with three thousand unarmed men, a large wagon train, and hundreds of cattle, thoroughly surrounded by more than 20,000 of the enemy (which General Hurlbut admits in his official report), having to cross three overflowed rivers, with the loss of less than thirty men, seems marvelous. And almost any other man, to have thought of such a possibility, would have been regarded as foolishly rash and perilously vain.

A correspondent of the *Cincinnati Commercial*, writing from Memphis on January 12, 1864, in summing up Forrest's operations, said: "With less than 4,000 men, Forrest moved right through the Sixteenth Army Corps, passed within nine miles of Memphis, carried off one hundred wagons of provisions, seven hundred head of beef cattle, and innumerable stores; tore up railroad track, cut telegraph wires, ran over our pickets with a single Derringer pistol, and all in the face of 20,000 men, and without the loss of a man that can be accounted for."

Arriving at Holly Springs, Forrest found that the almost incessant rain for a week was giving way to clear, cold weather.

On December 28 the command moved toward Como, Panola County, Miss. Forrest reached Sucotobia late Wednesday evening, December 30, and remained there until Friday morning, January 1, 1864, thence to Como.

Between Como and Senatobia runs the Hickahala River, which the entire command crossed, including the artillery and wagons, on the ice. It was the coldest day known to the oldest inhabitants, and will never be forgotten during the life of those who encountered its horrors.

The writer was ordered to move with a small squad of men as rapidly as possible ahead and press into service every ablebodied negro to be found and put them to work chopping down timber and building fires.

Arriving at Como, there was not a member of the little party able to dismount without assistance, but the few citizens and negroes of the town set to work to throw us out, and within a half hour or so we were able to begin the work. The men were scantily clad, and, with less than a blanket each, their suffering was fearful, so much so that numbers of the young recruits which followed out of West Tennessee left their commands to return home.

In the meantime, Forrest had been appointed a major general and put in command of all the forces in North Mississippi and West Tennessee. He set to work to organize his force into regiments and brigades. Four brigades were formed, the first under Brig. Gen. R. V. Richardson; the second under Col. Robert McCullough, composed of the 2nd Missouri, Willis's Texas Battalion, Faulkner's Kentucky Regiment, Kinzer's Battalion, the 18th Mississippi, and a fragment of the 2nd Arkansas, commanded by Capt. F. M. Cochran.

The third brigade was under Col. T. H. Bell, and the fourth was commanded by Col. J. E. Forrest, a brother of the General. In all, there were about 6,000 men, rank and file. The brigades commanded by Cols. McCullough and J. E. Forrest composed the first division, and it was commanded by Brig. Gen. James R. Chalmers. The other division was commanded by Brigadier General Richardson for a short time, but finally by Brig. Gen. A. Buford.

These details having been accomplished, Forrest moved his headquarters to Oxford, and left General Chalmers at Panola. While at Oxford, the squads which had been sent after the deserters returned with nineteen of them, whom they delivered to General Forrest. He gave orders that in consequence of this desertion and disgraceful conduct, the whole lot should be shot, and instructions were issued that the executions would take place at an early date. The news spread like a cyclone, and very soon prominent citizens and ladies, also every clergyman in Oxford, waited on General Forrest with urgent appeals to forgive the boys and spare their lives. Some of the officers advised Forrest that they had intimations of meetings among the soldiers. But he was unmoved, and apparently determined on the executions. All preparations were carried out, and on a bright morning, the 20th of January, 1864, the procession of wagons containing the deserters, sitting on their coffins, moved through the streets to a skirt of woods just west of the university buildings, where the graves had been dug. The men were made to get out, and the coffins placed alongside the graves. Then all were blindfolded and seated each on his coffin. The company detailed for the purpose marched in front and loaded their guns, and came to a ready. There was but a moment between these men and eternity. The next instant the commands "Aim" and "Fire" would be given. But while they were standing at the ready, Captain Anderson, of General Forrest's staff, announced that the men were pardoned and would return to their commands. The lesson was not lost, and will never be forgotten by anyone who was a witness to the spectacle. As a matter of fact, I do not know of more than a dozen men living who were present at that time. The news scattered broadcast that Forrest had shot a lot of boys who went home, etc., and many people believed to the day of their death that the boys were shot. The writer was present, and the statement is true in every particular as given above.

A short time after the occurrence just mentioned, General Polk, who was department commander, notified Forrest that Sherman was moving from Vicksburg toward Jackson, with a large force; also that a force had moved at the same time up the Yazoo River. This information was quickly followed by news that a column had moved from Memphis toward Panola, and another from Collinville toward Holly Springs.

Jeffrey Forrest was sent to Grenada to watch the column moving by the Yazoo River, while General Chalmers posted McCulloch at Panola, Bell at Belmont, and Richardson at Wyatt, all on the Tallahatchie River. Forrest soon learned however, that a large cavalry force was arranging to leave Memphis, and he at once decided that it was intended to participate in a coöperative movement with Sherman, and that the columns sent toward Panola and Holly Springs were feints.

Sure enough, on the 11th of February, Capt. Thomas Henderson, Chief of Scouts, reported that a force of cavalry about eight thousand strong and four batteries of artillery were moving rapidly in the direction of Germantown. Forrest ordered Chalmers to move with his division to Oxford, leaving one regiment (Falkner's) to guard the river at Wyatt and Abbeville.

Reaching Oxford on the 14th, Chalmers received orders to march with all dispatch toward Okolona, as the enemy, under Maj. Gen. W. S. Smith, about ten thousand strong, seemed headed for the rich prairies south of Okolona, which facts confirmed Forrest's opinions. It was raining almost constantly, and the roads were next to impassable, but we outmarched General Smith's force and reached West Point, Miss., on the 17th. Forrest established his headquarters at Starkville and sent Col. Jeffrey Forrest with his brigade to meet the Federal column in the neighborhood of Aberdeen.

Colonel Forrest had a number of light skirmishes while General Smith pressed his small brigade back to West Point. Anticipating that General Smith might cross the Tombigbee at Aberdeen, Bell's Brigade was sent to Columbus, where he crossed the river and moved along the east bank toward Aberdeen, but finding that Smith was moving his entire force toward West Point, he took up a position at Waverly. In the meantime, Forrest, with Chalmers, marched with McCulloch's Brigade and two regiments of Richardson's Brigade, to the relief of Col. Jeffrey Forrest.

The situation at this time was critical on both sides. The rivers in front and behind both the Federal and Confederate forces were badly swollen, and there could be no retreat for either. The Tombigbee on the east the Sooh-a-Toucha on the south, and the Okatibbyha on the west were all in flood.

Gen. Stephen D. Lee notified Forrest that he was marching to his support with a brigade of infantry from Meridian, and Forrest hoped to avoid a general engagement until his arrival. Forrest, therefore, went into camp about four miles west of West Point, from whence we could see the eastern horizon lighted up by burning houses, barns, gin houses, fences, and everything which the enemy could set on fire.

The sight so infuriated Forrest that he determined to put a stop to further devastation. The following morning he led McCulloch's Brigade to a crossing on a little river called Siloam, about four miles east, and resolved to do all in his power to stop such an uncivilized kind of warfare. He expected to strike the Federal left flank, but found that the force consisted of but one brigade, which he quickly put to flight. He ordered all his force forward from West Point, and found the enemy in position in a woods four miles from that little city.

Chalmers quickly dismounted his men and moved to the attack. The men went rushing and yelling at the Federal line with as little concern for their lives, apparently, as they would have shown in a skirmish drill. The effect was instantaneous, and the Federals, after firing a round, mounted their horses and galloped away.

In the meantime, McCulloch had sent the force at Siloam helter-skelter. The fugitives, on reaching Smith's main column, added tenfold to the demoralization. The whole force began a hurried retreat. Having the swollen river at their backs, the audacious onslaught of the Confederates made the victory a stampede. The Federals could not be halted. The scene was indescribable. The roads were knee deep in mud and the fields were boggy. Wagons and caissons were left behind, and our men could barely keep in sight of the fleeing house burners. Stop a moment and think of the disparity of the two forces.

General Smith's command numbered ten thousand men and twenty-four cannon. Men who had been selected from the Army of the Cumberland, seasoned and tried troops, with the best equipment, while Forrest's force did not exceed 4,000 men and eight cannon. Bell's Brigade of 2,000 men at Waverly, ten miles distant, when the fight began, did not reach the field until after the rout began. The roads and the whole country were soaked from the continued rain, and the passage of the Federal artillery and wagons left the roads impassable. Forrest made every effort to overhaul the enemy by sending detachments through the fields, but the ground was so rotten it could not be done, although the enemy was encumbered with plunder and hundreds of negroes.

However, Forrest was after them and with unsurpassed impetuosity succeeded in overtaking the Federal rear guard, several times during the day, with his escort company, and had two or three sharp brushes, but was not able to bring them to a stand.

Night coming on, the command went into camp, but the following morning, February 22, 1864, McCulloch's and Jeffrey Forrest's brigades were in hot pursuit.

Nine miles south of Okolona, Jeffrey Forrest was ordered to take a left-hand road, and cut off the retreat if possible. In the meantime Barteau, with Bell's Brigade, had reached the Federal right flank, which forced the enemy to make a stand at Okolona. Forrest, at the same time had been dogging the rear of the Federal column with his escort company so savagely there was no alternative but to fight. General Smith, therefore, posted his force in a very favorable position across the Pontotoc road, in a skirt of woods. Barteau, with Bell's Brigade, dismounted, charged across a field and met strong resistance and suffered great loss, but just at that moment Jeffrey Forrest struck the Federals in the rear, and caused another stampede. Barteau's men quickly recovered their setback and joined in pursuit. McCulloch reached the field about this time, and his presence added to the confusion of the Federals, and the rout became general. The Confederates, however, in the excitement, lost organization for a time and did not follow up the chase as well as could have been done. In the meantime, General Smith had found a most favorable position eight miles distant from Okolona, and posted his line on a ridge of post oak timber. Forrest soon got his men in hand and sent McCulloch to the left and Jeffrey Forrest to the right, with orders to drive into them. Jeffrey Forrest, at the head of his brigade, accompanied by Col. D. M. Wisdom, made the attack with great vigor. The Federals fired a volley into his ranks as he approached and Colonel Forrest fell, mortally wounded, about fifty yards from the enemy's line. The enemy was pushed back, and soon General Forrest, hearing of the wounding of his young brother, galloped to the spot where he lay, dismounted, raised his head, and with passionate tenderness begged Jeffrey to speak. He died in his arms. They were throughout life devoted. The General was the oldest and Jeffrey was the youngest of the family. The general had been unwearied in his efforts to give his brother an education, and he felt his untimely loss. The flower of his life had been snatched from him.

Laying down the body, Forrest spread his handkerchief over his dead brother's face and, calling on a member of his escort to remain with the corpse, he mounted his horse and said to those who were present: "Follow me." Then turning to his bugler, he said, "Garis, sound the charge," and away he dashed, followed by those present, with the fury of a hurricane. They galloped into the enemy as some of them were mounting to retreat, and the spirit and animation of the spectacle so enthused the other Confederates that they rushed forward like a mighty storm and trampled down everything in their front, driving the enemy in the wildest confusion and capturing all his artillery, wagons, and a thousand prisoners, besides a great quantity of supplies and several hundred negroes, who were running away with the Yankees. The pursuit was kept up until night. It was a wonderful achievement.

I was induced to write this story because of a remark made to me by an old comrade I met during the reunion of the Louisiana Division, U. C. V., held at Alexandria, November 25-26. He said: "Forrest's Cavalry was the greatest body of soldiers ever assembled:" I answered: "They were made so by Forrest's example."

SIGNERS OF THE DECLARATION OF INDEPENDENCE.

JOHN HANCOCK, MASSACHUSETTS.

Among the many striking characters of the fifty-six signers of the Declaration of Independence is John Hancock, president of the Continental Congress and the first to affix his signature to the document.

He was a graduate of Harvard, a wealthy man and a courtly figure; gold and silver adorned his garments, and on public occasions his carriages, horses and servants in livery emulated the splendor of the nobility. His mansion displayed the magnificence of the courtier rather than the simplicity of a republican. Rivaling the British in the gorgeousness of his attire, John Hancock was in striking contrast to the colonists, who effected a plain mode of dress. Because of these tendencies, doubts of his patriotic integrity were circulated.

John Hancock was an eloquent orator, and in commemoration of the Boston Massacre he delivered such a stirring speech no doubt was left in the mind of anyone as to his perfect patriotism. Hancock from this time became as odious to the royal governor and his adherents as he was dear to the Republican party. By this speech he put his life in jeopardy.

The British were determined to capture him, and we all know what his fate would have been had their efforts proved successful. John Hancock was spared to render his country splendid service. In promoting the liberties of his country he unstintingly expended great wealth and was willing to make many sacrifices. At the time the American army was besieging Boston, the destruction of Boston was considered. By the execution of these plans Hancock's whole fortune would have been sacrificed. Yet he immediately acceded to the measure and declared his readiness to surrender his all should his country require it.

His memory as one of the immortal signers of the Declaration, who pledged for their country's sake their lives, their fortunes and their sacred honors, is a cherished ideal in the hearts of all Americans.

BUTTON GWINNETT.

Twenty-two thousand five hundred dollars was the price paid recently for an autograph of Button Gwinnett, one of the three Georgia signers of the Declaration of Independence. His autograph is said to be the rarest of any of the fifty-six signers.

Gwinnett, the son of a minister, was born in England in 1732. He received a good education and was not illiterate as is commonly supposed. He emigrated to America and settled in Savannah in 1775. Here he became a successful business man and planter. He purchased a plantation on St. Catharine's Island, off the coast of Georgia, procured a number of negro slaves, and gave his attention to agriculture.

Previous to 1775, Gwinnett had not taken an active part in politics, but the subsequent enthusiasm with which he maintained Colonial rights attracted the attention of his fellow citizens. At a meeting of the Provincial Assembly held in Savannah in January, 1776, he was appointed a representative in Congress, signed the Declaration, and in October was reëlected for the ensuing year.

In February, 1777, he was appointed a member of the State government and is said to have furnished the basis of the Constitution which was finally adopted. Within a year after his first appearance in public life, he was appointed President of the Provincial Council, the highest station in the province, through the death of Archibald Bullock. As commander in chief of the Army of Georgia, he headed the expeditions against the British forces occupying St. Augustine.

At the time when he represented Georgia in Congress, Gwinnett became candidate for brigadier general of the Continental brigade to be levied in Georgia in opposition to General Lachlan McIntosh, but was unsuccessful in the election. This defeat so embittered the signer that they were enemies ever afterwards. In a session of the Assembly, Gwinnett was insulted by McIntosh, and the former challenged him to a duel. They fought with pistols at a distance of twelve feet, both were wounded above the knee, and Gwinnett died shortly afterwards.—*From a series issued by the Sesqui-Centennial Publicity Department.*

WHEN GENERAL MULLIGAN WAS KILLED.

BY I. G. BRADWELL, BRANTLEY, ALA.

On the 24th of July, 1864, near Kernstown, a suburb of Winchester, Va., where more battles were fought during the war of the sixties than anywhere else in the South, occurred the death of James A. Mulligan, commanding Federal forces. He was a brave old Irishman, and, like many of his countrymen who were fighting on our side, lost his life for a cause he considered right. In one of these numerous engagements in the Valley between the Confederates under Early and the Yankees under Sheridan, we lost brave old Colonel Monahan, of the 5th Louisiana Regiment, at the time in command of his brigade. Too corpulent to keep up in a headlong charge, he always rode his splendid bay horse to carry him over ditches and rough ground. He was leading his men when a ball passed through his body and ended his career as a soldier of the Confederacy.

When Cleveland was elected President, he rewarded Mulligan's widow, who was living in Chicago at the time, by appointing her postmaster at that city in place of Mrs. Logan, widow of General Logan, who was very popular with his political party at the time.

After our demonstration against Washington, D. C., we retraced our route and waded the Potomac at White's Ferry into Virginia, and rested awhile at Leesburg. The next day we reëntered the Valley at Snicker's Gap and made our camps nearby in the open country. By some oversight, our officers neglected to leave any pickets in the Gap to guard against a sudden approach of the enemy, who were following after us to capture, if possible, our wagon trains.

Late in the afternoon of July 18, a large force of their cavalry, finding this place unoccupied, placed their artillery there and opened on the camp of Gordon's Brigade. Our men seized their arms and were ready to meet their attack; but another large force, at the same time having crossed the mountains farther to the north, advanced on us from that direction. These two divisions united, and we had quite a fight with them, which lasted till a late hour of the night. While we occupied their attention in front, General Rodes struck them unexpectedly on the flank and routed them, killing and capturing many of them. The next day we followed after them many miles to the north in a running fight, in which there were few casualties on our side.

But this was only a part of the enemy's plan. I suppose the authorities at Washington were exasperated by the boldness of General Early in his attack on the national capital, and they determined to send a large force to the Valley to capture him and his whole army. This, the main army, was advancing from Shepherdstown in Early's rear along the Valley Pike. As soon as he was made aware of this, Early began a retreat to the vicinity of Strasburg, where he rested his army two or three days and awaited developments.

In the meantime reënforcements for the Confederates arrived; and since the enemy had stopped their advance near Kernstown for some reason and did not show any disposition to fight, Early assumed the offensive and decided to capture General Mulligan and his army.

I don't know how many men he had, but from the length of his line of battle, which extended at least three miles, he must have had several divisions.

The enemy's line when we drew up in front of them extended from southwest to northeast about that distance. It was evident to the minds of the Confederates, as soon as the skirmishing began, that aggressive leadership was lacking in the ranks of the enemy, and that victory would be easy.

But that was not what Early wanted. It was his purpose to capture the whole force sent against him and show the authorities at Washington his contempt for their effort to take him and his army. His plan was to make a heavy demonstration along the whole line except on the enemy's extreme left, where General Breckinridge was to face on them in a rapid charge, so as to get into their rear, when the whole line would move forward and rout the enemy, thus cut off from any way of escape toward the Potomac and safety.

Everything was carried out according to the plan. Breckridge moved forward, and a bitter engagement began. The enemy was driven forward; and we who were facing Mulligan and his men on their extreme right could hear, far to the north, the angry rattle of musketry and the boom of artillery, and we knew that our men were far in the rear of those we were facing. We (Gordon's Georgia Brigade) were lying flat on our faces in a piece of woodland to avoid the fire of the enemy, while our skirmishers, concealed in a ravine below us, were having a lively time with those of our friend Mulligan over the way around a large handsome brick residence and apple orchard about the premises. This house must have been his headquarters, for here he was mortally wounded perhaps by the sharpshooters of Gordon's Brigade and taken into it, where he died that night. He must have endeared himself to the occupants of the house by his kindness to them, for we heard that his death was very much regretted by them and all who knew him.

But the noise of battle in their rear was a warning to the enemy in our front which they were not slow to heed, and they proved to us that they had as good legs as we had and knew how to use them when in a tight place. Seeing their lines beginning to waver, the whole Confederate force moved forward in a rush, but the fighting, though sharp, was over in a few minutes, for the enemy, after the wounding of their general, had lost heart and thought of nothing but making their way to the fords of the Potomac and safety in their fortified position on Maryland Heights. They managed to escape from Breckinridge in their rapid flight. We pursued them through Winchester to Stephenson's Depot, and then camped after dark. The cavalry pressed after them, now fleeing in great confusion, and found the road strewn with abandoned wagons, ambulances, dead horses, and every manner of army equipment.

As we rushed past the residence where Mulligan was lying wounded, we could hear him groaning, and we were told about the circumstance. Though an enemy, we could not refrain from sympathizing with him in his suffering, for he had the reputation of being a magnanimous foe.

General Mulligan had served early in the war out in Missouri against General Price, and, if I am not mistaken, was captured by the Confederates.

Among the soldiers of this army who saved themselves from capture with the greatest difficulty was Maj. William McKinley, who afterwards was elected President of the United States. It so impressed him that he never forgot his experience in this affair.

General Breckinridge's failure to push in a little farther so as to block the Valley Pike alone saved them.

What old Jube would have done with so large a bunch of prisoners at a time when all Southern prisons were overflowing with captives is a question.

LAST OF C. S. ORDNANCE DEPARTMENT.

BY JOSEPH R. HAW, HAMPTON, VA.
(Continued from December number.)

It was on Sunday, the 30th, after passing through Cross Keys and over the Enoree River, that we learned from a Kentucky soldier, seated on the yard fence in front of a farmer's residence, that Captain Williams, of the 9th Kentucky Regiment, had been killed in a fight with a civilian that morning, and that his body was in the house awaiting burial. When we came up with the brigade that night, I learned from Lieutenant Morgan something more of the affair, as his brother, Capt. Job M. Morgan, quartermaster of the 8th Tennessee, was a witness of the killing.

On May 1, we marched until near the Saluda River and went into camp to await our turn to be ferried across. At Abbeville we came up with the Confederate States treasure in charge of Capt. William H. Parker, Superintendent of the Confederate Naval Academy. The steamer Jamestown was the school ship and the home of the Academy. It was kept in James River between Richmond and Drewry's Bluff. On the 2nd of April, Captain Parker was ordered by the Secretary of the Navy, S. K. Mallory, to take charge of the Confederate treasure with his corps of midshipmen and entrain for Danville. From that time until the 2nd of May he had guarded it, conveyed it from Richmond to Danville, through North and South Carolina, into Georgia, and back to Abbeville by railroad and wagon train. Here, by order of Secretary Mallory, he turned it over to Gen. Basil Duke intact. Captain Parker, in his account of this trip, published in the *Richmond Dispatch*, July 16, 1893, pays a glowing tribute to his corps of officers and midshipmen for their discipline, integrity, and fidelity under the most trying circumstances. The corps consisted of officers besides Captain Parker: Captain Rochelle, Surgeon Garrison, Paymaster Wheeler, Lieutenants McGuire, Peek, Sanxy, and Armistead, and about sixty midshipmen. On the 4th of May, while still in camp near the Savannah River, we were paid off in specie. A blanket was spread on the ground, on which a bucket of Mexican silver dollars was distributed in little piles, one for each member of the company, twenty in each pile, and gold and small change added to make very nearly $26. Although I had been with them a very short time, they very kindly shared equally with me, giving me very nearly $26. Some years ago there were stories written about the disposal of this money which reflected on Wheeler's men. To refute these fictions, I will give as brief an account as possible of its disposal, quoting from M. H. Clark, whom I have already mentioned, and who was appointed by President Davis as Assistant Treasurer, and who acted as the last Treasurer of the C. S. A. government.

The whole amount of the treasure which, it appears, reached Charlotte, is put at $327,022. Major General Breckinridge took command of the troops at Abbeville and marched with them across the Savannah River. Dibrell's Brigade stopped near the river, while the others went on to Washington.

By request of the men, General Breckinridge stopped the train and took out $108,322.90, which, at $26 each, would pay off 4,166 men, and this was paid out on the next day, the 4th of May. Other payments included the President's guard, consisting of disabled Confederate soldiers commanded by three one-armed officers, Captain Coe, Lieutenants Brown and Dickinson, unattached officers; Captain Parker and the midshipmen and officers; a few men of the Marine Corps; a part of General York's Brigade, and many other government employees. President Davis ordered the specie silver, amounting to about $40,000, to be paid over to Major Moses, quartermaster, to buy rations for paroled soldiers on the way to their homes to relieve citizens of the burden of feeding them. Captain Clark says the last payment, made at Washington, Ga., was $86,000 in gold coin and bullion to a trusted naval officer to be taken out of the country to be held for the Treasury Department. In the article I have quoted from Captain Parker says that this was not done, that it was not taken out of the country, and that this money was not accounted for. No attack was ever made on the Confederate Treasury. It was guarded faithfully from Richmond to Washington, Ga., and nearly all of it disbursed there, nor did Mr. Davis receive any of it in person. The train was never with him. He found it at Abbeville and left it there, and Captain Clark says he did not pay out any money to him.

There was no rioting at Washington, though the town was filled with soldiers under no command. Money from the banks of Richmond, accompanied by the bank's officers, amounting to about $230,000 which had been with the train up to this time, was turned over to these officers. I have seen it stated that a mob captured this money and divided it among themselves; that the banks tried very hard to recover their money, but never did succeed.

We had learned on the 3rd that General Johnston had surrendered on the 26th of April, and that General Dibrell considered his division entitled to the same terms. On the 5th, we moved camp up the river to where the Broad flows into the Savannah, a beautiful camping ground in a grove of oaks and hickory, with bowlders of gray rock scattered through the wood and the river convenient for bathing. It was now generally known that the President had left the cavalry and that negotiations were now in progress for surrender. Men talked of going home and began to prepare for that event. Many of them expected to take up farm life again and raise horses for the then depleted market. With this end in view there was a lively trading of horses, and a mare that possessed the qualities of a breeder rose steadily in value, and many a silver dollar went in boot between a gelding and a mare, while the possessor of a large white stallion was the envy of the command. Going home to many of these Tennesseeans and Kentuckians was a rather serious business, as they would meet neighbors against whom they had been fighting for four years. Several of our company continued their journey to the Mississippi River and, no doubt, got over that stream. We remained in camp here until the morning of the 8th, when we marched to Washington, Ga., for the purpose of being paroled. There was a very small force of Yankees in the town, probably a company. Several of the best scribes were busy filling out the parole blanks. On the morning of the 10th, to my surprise, the bugler sounded "boots and saddles," and the command broke camp and moved out on the road to take up the line of march. The Federal officers having received orders to parole the divisions, allowing none to keep their horses save the officers, General Dibrell decided to march his men as near their homes as possible, so that they could disperse and retain their horses. Learning that some of the men who were dismounted were going to take their paroles and go home by rail, I rode my horse down to the provost marshal's office, and, in company with the dismounted men, got my parole. I then rode back to the company, bade them a long farewell, and turned my face homeward.

In 1866, I received a letter from Lieut. J. H. Morgan saying that at Chattanooga, Tenn., the men of Dibrell's command were halted and their horses taken from them by the Yankees; that an order was issued soon afterwards restoring the horses, but that many of them were not returned. Some years ago Congress appropriated $30,000 to pay for these horses that were thus taken contrary to the terms of the surrender of Lee and Johnston, and the men were reimbursed. Lieutenant Morgan became Attorney General of Tennessee and died about 1900.

Federal cavalry having torn up the road through South Carolina made it necessary for me to ride to Chester to take the train. I met Gen. Josiah Gorgas, Chief of Ordnance, in citizen dress, traveling in a one-horse spring wagon, drawn by the sorrel stallion which he had brought all the way from Richmond. The wagon seemed to be loaded with personal property. He stopped to make inquiries about the road, etc., which I answered as best I could, and we then passed on.

I spent the night in Abbeville, and on the 12th I passed through Cokesbury and crossed the Saluda at a ferry. Everything was very quiet as I rode through South Carolina. As a rule, the negroes had not left the plantations, and I could see them at work in the fields every day. I shall never forget these last views of a closing era. I remember passing a field of young corn across which there marched slowly, with hoes in hand, about twenty negro men and women, fighting grass. They were neatly dressed and kept the line dressed as straight as a company of soldiers. Behind them walked, with head erect and stately tread, a negro man clad in a dark Prince Albert coat, dark pants, white collar, and necktie. "You are having the work done?" I said. "Yes, sah, I am gwine to have some of it done." On Sunday the 14th I crossed Broad River. It was a quiet, bright Sabbath day, and along the road I could not help observing the order with which the negroes observed it. There was a group of negro quarters on the roadside, and the negroes were seated in front of them. Everything was in the best of order, the negro women dressed in neat, clean homespun checks, with clean white handkerchiefs tied turban fashion around their heads, all looking the picture of health and contentment. This was the last picture of the old time, for when I reached Virginia the liberty license idea had filled the negroes' heads and they had crowded to the cities.

Early in the afternoon I stopped at a house near Chester to get lunch and the lady gave me a slice of ham and a slice of bread. Her son, when I told him I would have to leave my horse, gave me a twenty-dollar bank note, stating solemnly that it was good Yankee money. As there was, for very good reasons, nothing better to do, I gave him the horse and Colt revolver for the bank note. This was just four weeks since I had, on Easter Sunday, "jined the cavalry." I entered Chester just before dark. The place was filled with paroled soldiers. I saw no Yankees. I took the train for Charlotte on Monday morning, May 15, and found my parole good for railroad fare to my home, as an order had been issued granting this privilege for sixty days to all paroled soldiers. At Charlotte I was joined by R. F. Bell, a young soldier of the 30th Virginia Regiment, on his way to his home in Spotsylvania County, Va. He was accompanied by a member of Barringer's Brigade, who had two very bad saber cuts on the head, received in a charge in the last fighting in Virginia. Bell was not yet eighteen years old. He was sick in a hospital in Richmond and paid a negro ten dollars to carry him on his back to the depot to leave the city, and kept going until he reached South Carolina.

In Charlotte I discovered that my twenty-dollar bank note would not pay for two drinks of lemonade; had to produce the hard specie. Learned here that some of Johnston's army received one dollar and fifteen cents pay in silver when paroled. On the 16th we took the train for Danville, where I found, to my disgust, that the train for Richmond in the morning would be a freight. Bell secured sleeping room on a flat car and made our blanket bed with a Pennsylvania Yankee returning home on furlough. The Yank was very happy and took a great liking to Bell. Thus was the bloody chasm spanned when two Rebel boys slept peaceably under the same blanket with a Yankee soldier. At Burkville Junction we took the top of a box car on a freight train for Petersburg, arriving just before night. Early the next morning I went out on the street to buy something to eat. The town was patrolled by Yankee sentinels at almost every square. The first one halted me and asked if I had a knife. I asked him what he wanted with it, and he said "to cut those military buttons off!" said I could cut them off or go to see the provost marshal. I had at some expense and trouble procured Virginia State buttons and valued them very highly, so I started for the provost marshal's office, and as soon as out of the sight of the sentinel, cut them off and put them in my pocket. This was a general order, and many paroled soldiers evaded it by covering the brass buttons with cloth. Many of us had no change of citizen's clothes to wear. On the 18th Bell and I took train for Richmond. At Manchester we found the bridges burned, and we crossed on a pontoon bridge. At Franklin Street I met my one-armed brother, Lieut. George P. Haw, on his way to Newport News prison camp and hospital to visit my brother William, who had been desperately wounded at Five Forks and was confined in that camp, called the "Bull Pen." Bell and I remained in Richmond that night and on the 19th walked about the town to see the effects of the fire. We found a good part of Main and Cary Streets in ruins and Yankee sentinels at almost every square. Numbers of negroes were loafing on the streets, having come in to town to fully realize their freedom. On the 20th of May we took train on the Virginia Central Railroad (now the Chesapeake and Ohio) for our homes. R. F. Bell was a brother of J. B. Bell, bookbinder, stationer, etc., of Lynchburg, Va. He died in that town about 1903.

SOUTH CAROLINA'S REPRESENTATIVES IN THE CONFEDERATE CONGRESS.

SKETCHES COMPILED BY MRS. A. A. WOODSON, EDGEFIELD, S. C.

When the First Provisional Congress of the Confederacy met in Montgomery, Ala., in 1861, the delegates from South Carolina were W. Barnwell Rhett, Christopher G. Memminger, William Porcher Miles, James Chestnut, Jr., Robert W. Barnwell, William W. Boyce, Lawrence M. Keitt, and Thomas J. Withers. When the President for the infant government was chosen, the vote of the entire delegation was for Jefferson Davis, and all of these gentlemen were likewise present at the signing of the Constitution which, while it was formulated on lines adopted by the Constitution of the United States, differed from it in several vital points. South Carolina was allowed two Senators and six Representatives, and the Senators chosen were Robert W. Barnwell and James M. Orr.

Dr. J. L. M. Curry, writing of the Constitutional Convention, says: "The Constitution of the Confederate States as the instrument of government is the most certain and decisive expression of the views and principles of those who formed it, and it is entitled to credence and acceptance as the most trustworthy and authoritative exposition of the principles and purposes of those who established the Confederate government."

It is concerning the members of that Congress and their compeers of the permanent Congress who represented South Carolina, however, that we purpose to write. Representatives chosen for the permanent Confederate Congress were James L. Orr, Senator; Lewis Malone Ayer, Armistead Burt, W. D. Simpson, M. L. Bonham, Jehu A. Orr, and James H. Witherspoon. The permanent Congress of the Confederate States met in Richmond, Va., on February 22, 1862, and declared Jefferson Davis elected President for a term of six years.

Robert Barnwell Rhett, a native of Charleston and a member of that large and distinguished family which has held positions of honor and trust in the State and had worked for her best interests, was sent as a delegate to the convention which resulted in the organization of the Confederate government and the naming of the President. Howell Cobb, of Georgia, was nominated by Rhett to be president of the Provisional Congress, and Rhett himself was made chairman of a committee to draw up a constitution, the directions being that it must conform to the Constitution of the United States as nearly as possible. Thomas R. R. Cobb, of Georgia, a member of that committee, wrote the Constitution of the Confederate States, and the original draft in Mr. Cobb's handwriting is to be seen in the University of Georgia. This first Provisional Congress adjourned March 16, 1861, to meet again in May. The second session, which was a called session, met in Montgomery, April 29, 1861, and adjourned May 21, 1861. Robert Barnwell Rhett, who had previous to hostilities, served in both Houses of the United States Congress, was defeated for reëlection from the third South Carolina district by Gen. Lewis Malone Ayer. Of Rhett, Gen. James Chestnut said: "He was a very bold and frank man, one who was not afraid to avow his opinions and act upon them." In the First Provisional Congress he voted for Mr. Davis for President and Mr. Stephens for Vice President.

Christopher Gustavus Memminger, afterwards Secretary of the Treasury in President Davis's cabinet, also attended that First Provisional Congress in Montgomery. He was born in Wurtemburg, Germany, on January 7, 1803, and was brought to America as an infant. At four years of age he was left an orphan and was placed in the Charleston Orphanage. From there he was adopted by Mr. Thomas H. Bennett, reared and educated carefully, graduating at the South Carolina College. He chose the profession of law and for nearly twenty years was chairman of the finance committee of the South Carolina House of Representatives. At Montgomery he drafted the Constitution of the Confederate States of America, and upon the organization of the government was appointed by Mr. Davis as Secretary of the Treasury.

William Porcher Miles, a third distinguished delegate, was the son of James F. Miles and his wife, Sarah Bond Warley, daughter of Felix Warley of Revolutionary fame. He was born on July 4, 1822, and educated at Willington Academy in Abbeville County and at the College of Charleston, where he graduated with first honors. Studied law, served as mayor of Charleston, and was a member of the National House of Representatives, 1856-1858-1860. He was elected a member of the Secession Convention of South Carolina, signing the famous ordinance in December, 1860, and was made chairman of Foreign Relations. He was chosen as a deputy from South Carolina to the Constitutional Convention, and upon the organization of the government of the Confederate States, he was elected a member of its Congress from Charleston district and in that body was chairman of the Military Committee. During the bombardment of Fort Sumter, he acted as a volunteer aide to General Beauregard. He was chairman of the Flags and Seals Committee in the Provisional Congress, and planned to use a St. Andrew's Cross, his design being one of the four submitted to Congress. After the war he went to Virginia, having married a daughter of Oliver Berne, Esq., of that State. He resided in Nelson County until he was called back to South Carolina to be president of the South Carolina College in 1883. Later he moved to Louisiana.

In Kershaw County may still be seen the lovely old home of the Chestnuts, where lived Gen. James Chestnut, Jr., a descendant of the Kershaw family. His ancestors, among whom were Joseph Kershaw and John Chestnut, first settled in Charleston and afterwards pushed up into the interior. James Chestnut served during Nullification Days on the staff of Gov. Stephen D. Miller, whose daughter, Mary, became his wife. As a volunteer aide on Beauregard's staff, he was chosen by that officer to go with the committee demanding the surrender of Fort Sumter from General Anderson. As a member of the Constitutional Congress, he was one of the signers of the Confederate Constitution. He was later chosen to serve on the staff of President Davis. Writing of the election of Davis and Stephens, he said: "Before leaving home, I had made up my mind as to who were the fittest men to be President and Vice President, Mr. Davis and Mr. Stephens." Chestnut had been a member of the United States Senate from South Carolina, 1859-60, and was associated with these two in Washington.

Immediately after the secession of the State, the convention of South Carolina deputized three distinguished citizens—Robert W. Barnwell, James H. Adams, and James L. Orr—to proceed to Washington and treat with the government of the United States for the delivery of forts, magazines, and lighthouses "with their appurtenances within the limits of South Carolina, etc., and for the continuance of peace and amity between the commonwealth and the government at Washington." Robert W. Barnwell later became Senator in the Confederate Congress, first in Montgomery, and then in Richmond. Writing of him, William Porcher Miles says: "If I were to select anyone as having special influence with us, I would consider Mr. Robert W. Barnwell as the one. His singularly pure and elevated character, entire freedom from all personal ambition or desire for place or position, as well as his long experience in public life and admirably calm and well-balanced mind, all combined to make his influence with his colleagues very great. But neither could he be said to lead the delegation. He had no desire and never made any attempt to do so." President Davis wrote: "It was my wish that Robert W. Barnwell, of South Carolina, should be Secretary of State. I had known him intimately during a trying period of our joint service in the United States Senate, and he won alike my esteem and regard. Before making known to him my wish in this connection, the delegation from South Carolina, of which he was a member, had resolved to reconmmend one of their number to be Secretary of the Treasury, and Mr. Barnwell, with characteristic delicacy, declined to accept my offer to him." Mr. Barnwell was a member of President Davis's personal staff at the time of his capture.

William W. Boyce was a son of Robert W. Boyce, of Newberry County, his grandfather, John Boyce, emigrating to the United States from Ireland in 1765. He married Elizabeth Miller and served in the Revolution, the son Robert (father of

William W.) marrying Lydia Waters, daughter of the famed Philemon Waters. William W. Boyce was a prominent lawyer of Fairfield County when he was called to the service of the Confederacy. In 1858 and 1859 he had been a representative in the National Congress, and in 1861 was elected to the Confederate Congress from Fairfield District. As a member of the Constitutional Congress he was a signer of the Constitution.

Lawrence M. Keitt is best known in South Carolina as a brave officer of the Confederacy who made the supreme sacrifice. He was born in Orangeburg, October 4, 1824; was graduated from the South Carolina College in 1843, and admitted to the bar in 1845. He served in the State legislature in 1848, and was elected to the United States Congress in 1852 as a State Rights Democrat. He resigned his seat in Congress upon the withdrawal of his State from the Union, and was sent as a delegate to the Provisional Congress in Montgomery, where he was conspicuous in forming the permanent congress and Constitution. In 1862 he entered the Confederate army, and served gallantly as colonel of the 20th Regiment, South Carolina Volunteer Infantry. At the battle of Cold Harbor he was mortally wounded, and died in Richmond on the following day, June 4, 1864.

Thomas J. Withers was born in 1804 at Ebenezer, in York County. His father was Randolph Withers, of Virginia, and his mother a Miss Bailey. He became a journalist and a personal friend of Gov. Stephen D. Miller, the great exponent of nullification in South Carolina. Withers was a strong advocate of State Rights, and in 1861 was brought into active service as a delegate from South Carolina to the Provisional Congress. He died that same year.

James Lawrence Orr was born at Craytonville, Anderson County, S. C., May 12, 1822. He was educated at the University of Virginia, studied law, established and edited the *Gazette* at Anderson, opposed nullification, became prominent in politics, and served in the United States Congress for five consecutive terms. For sixteen years he opposed secession, but when that issue became a fact in South Carolina, he went with his State and was one of the commissioners sent by the State to treat with President Buchanan. In December, 1861, he was elected Senator from South Carolina to the Confederate Congress, having previously been in command of a regiment in the field. In February, 1862, he went to Richmond to take his seat, and served until the end. He was the first governor of his State elected after the close of the war, and it is a peculiar fact that during his term of office (1865–66), South Carolina was under two governments—military, under Canby, and civil, under Orr. He was deposed under act of the Federal government, later became circuit court judge, and in 1872 was appointed by President Grant as United States Minister to Russia. He died in St. Petersburg, while in service, May 5, 1873.

Lewis Malone Ayer, ex-Senator of the United States, and a member of the Confederate Congress, was born November 12, 1821. He is said to have walked three miles to school when a small boy, and at twelve years of age was sent to Edgefield to attend the old Male Academy, where he spent two years, later attending school in Winnsboro. He graduated from the South Carolina College in 1838, and at the University of Virginia in 1841, the following year receiving his diploma from the Harvard Law School. He practiced law at Barnwell Courthouse, was elected to the State legislature in 1848 and 1852, and in 1853 was made brigadier general of the Third Military District of South Carolina. In 1860 he was chosen to represent his district in the United States Congress, but on the secession of South Carolina, he resigned his seat and came home to assist in forming the new government. He was a member of the Secession Convention and signed the ordinance. In 1861, he was elected to the Confederate Congress from the same district, defeating Gen. D. F. Jamison, who had been president of the Secession Convention. In 1863, he was reëlected to Congress, defeating Hon. R. Barnwell Rhett, and served in this body until the close of the war.

Armistead Burt was a prominent lawyer in his adopted town of Abbeville and a life-long friend of the great statesman, John C. Calhoun. A half century ago, Mr. Burt played a large part in the making of South Carolina; now he lies in an unmarked grave in old Trinity Episcopal Church yard in Abbeville, where he died in 1883. He was born in old Edgefield District, November 16, 1802, and in his youth was taken to old Pendleton, where he was educated at the excellent academy there. He was elected to the United States Congress from Abbeville District in 1841, serving until he retired in 1852. He practiced law in Abbeville until the day when a mass meeting was held on "Secession Hill" in his town, participating in the deliberations of that meeting. After secession had been determined upon, he was sent as an envoy to Mississippi to ask that State to unite in forming the Confederacy. He was elected to the Confederate Congress and ably served, and it was in his home in Abbeville that the last meeting of the Confederate cabinet was held, there being present President Davis, Secretary of War John C. Breckinridge, Secretary of State Judah P. Benjamin, Secretary of the Navy S. R. Mallory, and Postmaster General John H. Reagan. Armistead Burt was with the President on his departure from Richmond, and a member of the family of the writer remembers this occurrence.

Judge W. D. Simpson was born in Laurens, S. C., October 27, 1823. He graduated with distinction from the South Carolina College in 1843 and studied one year at the Harvard Law School. He married a daughter of the Hon. Henry Young, one of the most prominent and successful lawyers of the Western Circuit. Before the war, Simpson represented Laurens County in the legislature several times, and was a member of the State Senate when the State seceded from the Union. In the beginning of the war he was at the siege of Fort Sumter as an aide on General Bonham's staff. After the first battle of Manassas, he returned to Laurens, where he was elected major in the 14th South Carolina Regiment, of which he afterwards became lieutenant colonel. He participated in the battles of Bull Run, Seven Days' Fight, Cold Harbor, Frazier's Farm, Malvern Hill, and Harper's Ferry, before being called home to represent South Carolina in the Confederate Congress, succeeding M. L. Bonham, who had been elected governor of the State. In 1876, he went into office as lieutenant governor with Hampton, assisting in casting off radical rule in South Carolina.

Gov. Milledge L. Bonham, son of James Bonham, was born in that section of old Edgefield which is now Saluda County, on May 6, 1815. He was graduated from the South Carolina College in 1835 with second honors, and studied law, but was soon called to serve his country as a member of the staff of General Bull in the Seminole War. He was admitted to the bar in 1837, and in the Mexican War served as colonel of the 12th Regiment of Infantry. On his return to Edgefield, he was made solicitor for the Southern Circuit, serving 1848-50. In the meantime he had become a major general in the State Militia. In 1856 he was elected to the United States Congress, resigning in 1860 on the secession of his State. Upon secession he was detailed as major general to command South Carolina troops, and was later appointed brigadier general in the Confederate army. He was in command of forces at First Manassas, but was called home to serve as a representative in the Confederate Congress, and in 1862 was chosen governor of the State. At the expiration of his term he returned, in 1864, to the army, serving again as brigadier general. He represented Edgefield in the State legislature, 1865–66. He married Ann Patience Griffin, daughter of N. L. Griffin, Edgefield lawyer and statesman. He died in 1890, and is buried at the Bonham place on the Saluda River.

Judge Jehu A. Orr was the youngest son of Christopher and Martha McCann Orr, and was born at Craytonville, Anderson County. He held the commission of colonel in the Confederate army and served as a member of the Confederate Congress. After the war he moved to Mississippi, where he became a circuit judge.

James H. Witherspoon, a member of the Confederate Congress, was a descendant of the prominent South Carolina family of that name which settled in Williamsburgh District and among the Waxhaws. He gave able service as a member of the House of Representatives of the Confederacy.

References for Study.—Cyclopedia of Eminent and Representative Men of the Carolinas, Volume I; Chapman's History of Edgefield County; Davis's Rise and Fall of the Confederate Government; Miller's Almanac of Eminent Men; Woodrow Wilson's History of the American People; The South in the Building of the Nation; The Library of Southern Literature; South Carolina Division, U. D. C. Catechism of Confederate History; Miss Rutherford's Scrapbook; O'Neall's Annals of Newberry; J. L. M. Curry's Southern States in the American Union.

[NOTE.—The call came to the Historian of the South Carolina Division, U. D. C. for the above information when she was on the eve of departing for the Richmond convention, which was to be almost immediately followed by the South Carolina Division convention. She called upon Mrs. Agatha A. Woodson, a faithful lover of Confederate history and former Historian of the Edgefield Chapter, to come to the rescue and her prompt response is gratefully appreciated.—MARION SALLEY, *Historian South Carolina Division.*]

EXPERIENCES OF A WAR-TIME GIRL.

BY MRS. JOHN P. SELLMAN, FREDERICK, MD.

Early in July, 1864, my friend, Mrs. White, wife of Col. E. V. White, commanding the 35th Battalion of Virginia Cavalry, C. S. A., called at the home of my father, Mr. C. T. Hempstone, near Leesburg, Va., to invite me to spend a few days with her at "Temple Hall," the home of Mr. Henry Ball, where Mrs. White, her children, and nurse, stayed for many months, just as they did at my father's home. That afternoon we planned a little trip across the Potomac River into Montgomery County, Md. The Yankee pickets having been withdrawn from the "Banks of the Potomac," we deemed it safe to make the trip to procure clothing for our dear Maryland boys in gray. With Betty and Kate Ball and their brother George we went in a two-horse open wagon to the home of Mrs. White's mother, Mrs. Gott, of Gott's Mill, near Dickerson. In the afternoon George Ball returned home, and Mrs. White's brother, John Gott, and I went on horseback to the home of Mr. and Mrs. Robert Sellman, near Clarksburg, who gave us cloth and boots. Their two sons were in the Confederate army, Alonzo being in White's 35th Battalion, and Wallace in Company A, 1st Maryland Cavalry. Soon afterwards Wallace died in the Valley of Virginia of typhoid fever.

On the outskirts of Barnesville we stopped at the home of Cap. and Mrs. William O. Sellman, whose oldest son, John Poole, ran away in the spring of 1861 from Brookville Academy where he was a student, and crossed the Potomac into Virginia to fight for State Rights and constitutional liberty. He joined Company K, 1st Virginia Cavalry. After serving in it one year, he and eighteen other young men met at Hanover Junction, Va., and organized Company A, 1st Maryland Cavalry, which was the nucleus of one of the most famous cavalry commands in the Confederate army.

Capt. William Sellman's daughter, Mary Jane, slipped a bundle of calico under my saddle as I sat on my horse, and we returned to Mrs. Gott's and spent the night. The next day we tied the cavalry boots to our hoop skirts and wound the cloth and calico in and out until we were burdened with weight. Thinking all was safe for our return, we started for home, but before reaching the Potomac we learned that pickets had been placed there again. Our hearts were full, and we trembled in fear of losing our treasured collection. We returned to Mrs. Gott's and hastened to secrete our much-valued articles by stringing them on ropes and suspending them in cuddy holes in the wall. We made ourselves comfortable, trusting for an early opportunity to return to Virginia, but ere the lapse of another day, Mrs. White was arrested by order of Major Thompson and taken to Muddy Branch, where she was stationed. Late that night he sent an ambulance with four guards for the Ball girls and me. It was well after midnight when we joined Mrs. White. We spent the rest of the night in a guarded house, which was infested with vermin. We kept our tallow dip burning, but the pests swarmed all the more. Early next morning we were taken in an ambulance to Washington and placed in Capitol Prison in close confinement, as we were accused of being spies and were threatened with hanging. Mrs. White and I were in room No. 41. Our furniture consisted of iron cots with straw beds; the rough gray blankets we hung at the window to shade our eyes from the glaring sun. While there, kind friends living in Washington visited us and did what they could to make us comfortable. I still have several cards that came with baskets of fruit and delicacies, which I shared with the soldiers confined in Capitol Prison.

Mrs. White was taken ill, and, as soon as she was able, was moved to a boarding house, and I was sent to nurse her. A Dr. Ford attended her. After three weeks we were paroled and given a pass. We first went to the home in Georgetown of a Mr. Williams, a relative of Mrs. White, who brought us in his carriage to Rockville, a distance of twelve miles, where we dined with Mrs. Bouie, and then went on to Mrs. Gott's. There we obtained our same collection of supplies and left for home, notwithstanding the Potomac was heavily guarded. Mr. Gott took us to Edward's Ferry as the safest place to cross the river. Mr. Will Jones, who was clerking in a store there, came out to help us out of the wagon. As he lifted me, I whispered; "Lift me down carefully, or my hoops may tilt and show the boots and materials."

The many letters I received from soldier friends while in prison I was unwilling to give up, so, in packing my valise, I placed them on top, that they might be seen by the Yankee guards who would search our baggage. When they opened my valise and the letters rolled out by the dozen, which I purposely arranged to aggravate the inspector, I laughed, which was considered a great insult, and he exclaimed in anger: "If I had my way, I would send you straight back to prison where you came from."

We crossed the Potomac in a skiff. I was obliged to stand, on account of the cavalry boots dangling from my hoop skirt. When we reached the Virginia shore, we walked to a house on

Goose Creek, where we had dinner, I have forgotten the name of the people, but they kindly sent us in a one-horse wagon to my home at Leesburg, where we were heartily welcomed by our loved ones. In a few days, our dear boys in gray of Colonel White's Battalion, hearing of our return, came to see us in my father's home, and we distributed the supplies we had collected.

It was in the Episcopal Church in Leesburg that I first saw John Poole Sellman; he was with Mr. Horatio Trundle. My sister Jennie whispered to me: "There is Johnny Sellman." That evening he came to my father's home and spent the night, leaving the next morning for Charlottesville to join the army. In October, after my return from prison, Mr. Sellman procured a furlough and came to Leesburg to spend a few days, and while at my father's home, a squad of Yankees invaded the town. Hearing they were near, he mounted his horse and fled to a near-by corn field, where he was captured, taken to Old Capitol Prison, and placed in close confinement, under threat of being hanged. In February, he was sent to Old Point Comfort, and from there on to Richmond to be exchanged.

While in prison Johnny Sellman took from his tin cup of soup a small beef bone, from which he made with his penknife a Maltese Cross, carving his initials upon it, and filling them with red sealing wax, using a common brass pin to make pin and catch, so that he might wear the cross on his coat. This cross is now one of my most cherished possessions. On February 13, 1866, I married him, and we lived near Barnesville until his death in 1908, after which, with my two daughters, I came to live in Frederick, Md. My only son, his father's namesake, lives in Washington, Ind.

In 1862 I made a small Confederate flag, the "Stars and Bars," for Mr. Sellman, which he carried through the war. It was used by my little grandson, Hunton Dade Sellman, when he helped unveil the Confederate monument in Rockville, Md., on June 3, 1913.

After the battle of Manassas, July 21, 1861, the 13th, 17th, 18th, and 21st Mississippi Regiments and the 4th South Carolina Regiment encamped near Leesburg until March 7, 1862. As soon as they arrived, several boys who were ill of typhoid fever were brought to my father's home and remained for weeks. Among them were Adjutant Nicholson, 18th Mississippi; Tip Williams, Charles Russell, and Capt. Edward Fontaine, all of Company K, 18th Mississippi. Captain Fontaine was an Episcopal clergyman, and preached one Sunday in St. James Church, Leesburg. When able to leave us, he received a furlough and went home, unfit for active service.

After the battle of Ball's Bluff, October 21, 1861, a hospital was established in the clerk's office in Leesburg, where my mother frequently went with one of her servants to carry food and minister to the comfort of the wounded and dying soldiers. In this battle, Jack Pettus, son of the governor of Mississippi, Mr. Halloway, Mr. Terrett, and others of Company K, 18th Mississippi, were killed. They were buried in Leesburg cemetery, and my sister and I took care of their graves. The best of all we had was kept for "our boys in gray."

Our growing crops were destroyed by the Yankees, fields of wheat just ready to harvest were trampled down, hogs butchered, and horses driven off. Several times there were threats to burn our home.

I was a young girl then, now I am in my eighty-third year, but have never forgotten the horrors of the War between the States, nor my love for the Confederacy.

WHEN CHRISTMAS CAME TO JOURNEY'S END.

BY BEATRICE KENT, OAK PARK, ILL.
(Continued from December.)

"Rest, sleep," her voice was tremulous. "I will return to-morrow."

How she got through that evening Anne never could tell. She only knew that she ran every step of the way back to the house and sped up to her own room where she sat wide-eyed, hands tightly clenched, and forgetful of time until Mary Vaill came anxiously to inquire if she was ill.

Then the Vance pride came to her aid, and she laughed away Mary's fears as she rearranged her disordered attire and once more a glorious, shimmering vision descended the broad staircase and rejoined her guests.

Dawn was breaking when the final adieux were spoken and all had departed except the house guest. Anne, at her father's side, bade each a smiling farewell. Then with a hasty kiss she left her astonished parent staring as she sped up the staircase.

In her own room she found Drucie, her black maid, and still with the new, grave, wondering mood upon her she allowed Drucie to remove the elegant ball gown and place about her shoulders a soft blue negligee with snowy swansdown trimmings. Lounging in a great carved chair before the fire, she lay back dreamily while the girl unbound the shining copper-gold hair and let it fall a gleaming mantle over her shoulders. Even the entrance of Mary Vaill, who was to share her room because of the crowded condition of the house, failed to arouse her, and her apathetic replies nearly drove the black-eyed, raven-haired beauty frantic.

"I do declare, Anne," she cried in vexation, "you are provoking. Whatever can ail you that you are so abstracted. Never tell me you are not smitten of Captain John. None but a girl in love would act as you do."

Anne started. A wave of crimson swept from throat to brow. She turned a frightened gaze upon Mary, which fortunately the latter failed to see and with an effort roused herself and feverishly chattered airy nothings and bits of gossip about the ball.

After a night of restless turnings and troubled dreams Anne woke to a world of gloom. Dark storm-filled clouds hung over a chilly world, until the atmosphere reflected the sullen sky. A light fall of snow blanketed the countryside and a penetrating dampness crept into one's very marrow.

The promise made the previous night weighed heavily upon Anne. No thought of not keeping it ever occurred to her. She had told the delirious highwayman that she would visit him on the morrow, and the promise would be fulfilled. But how? All day she sought a chance in vain. The guests at Journey's End (and there were many) roved about everywhere. They seemed to be especially interested in the guardhouse and its suffering occupant. A whispered inquiry of Dustin informed Anne that the prisoner was still "mighty sick." It was after dinner that evening that the first opportunity occurred. Mary Vaill, at the spinet, was delighting an admiring circle, Captain John and others were playing at cards. The opportunity had come. Hastily snatching a long cape from her room Anne threw it over her shoulders and, opening the side door sped down the path to the guardhouse. The barred door, was closed, but upon peering through then arrow paneled opening Anne discovered Dustin dozing in a chair. She softly called his name, and he sprang hastily to his feet and removed the fastenings. The heavy door swung open with a grinding sigh. Anne entered.

She bent over the sick man timidly. His eyes were open, but showed no recognition. She spoke scarcely above a whisper.

"Are you feeling bettter?" There was no reply. She looked at Dustin inquiringly.

"He's been that-a-way all day, Missy. Seems like he cain't rouse hisself."

"Is he worse?"

"Dunno. Capt. John Vance came to see him this mawning and talked to him about the awful crime he committed, and, though I don't know what was said, 'cause I warn't heah all de time, this robber got sort o' violent, and after Captain John left I found him lying on the floor, and I reckon he must er hurt hisself, 'cause he had a big bruise on his haid."

She turned again to the sick man.

"How could such a man be a robber, Dustin?" she spoke more to herself than to the freedman. Her soft, white hand passed lightly over the robber's head, smoothing back the silky brown hair. She bent over him, her lips close to his ear.

"Won't you rouse yourself? It is Anne speaking."

"Anne?" the name came thickly, in a whisper, "Anne, don't let him come near me again."

"You mean Capt. John Vance?"

"Yes," it was a gasp.

"Captain Vance will not harm you." Anne was much troubled at the turn the conversation had taken. "You are now my father's prisoner, not Captain Vance's. Some day you will be taken away from Journey's End and"—

The robber interrupted her.

"Don't let them take me away until after Christmas, promise, promise."

"I cannot. But I am sure you will not be removed until next week at the earliest. To-morrow will be Christmas Eve, and then"—

"Great God, so soon," he half rose. "Mistress Anne, will you leave me? I must think. O, that my brain were clear."

Anne turned in amazed and offended dignity.

"Sir," she began haughtily. The robber held out a hand. "I beg of you, bear with me," he said huskily, "I suffer mentally and physically."

She did not doubt him. Great pity welled into her heart, her eyes, her voice.

"Won't you let me help you?"

"You have, more than you realize. Mistress Anne, why have you been so good to me?"

"Why—why—because you were ill. I could not help it." She felt confused.

A strangely tender light came into the brown eyes.

"Mistress Anne, we do many things because we cannot help it."

"I must go," Anne drew her cape about her. The stranger held out his hand. Perforce she laid her own within it. Slowly, deferentially, he raised it to his lips, and the lingering pressure thrilled her. She, always so proud and defiant, felt like a child before this man. The glance she gave him was almost timid.

"Dustin, see your mistress to the house," there was a ring of authority in the command. The incongruity of a prisoner ordering his jailer about did not seem to occur to any of them. Anne passed out, followed by Dustin.

As she vanished up the brick paved walk a tall soldierly figure glided out of the shadows and entered the guardhouse. He gazed earnestly at the robber, now lying inert with closed eyes. A few moments' scrutiny seemed to satisfy him, and he touched the sick man lightly on the shoulder. The brown eyes opened and looked up in astonishment. The newcomer bent over him.

"I was not mistaken this morning," he said in a tone of triumph, "I thought I had seen you before. It was at Mini-sink and prisoners had been brought in—deserters trying to join the British"—

"Who are you?" asked the sick man. The stranger bent and whispered a name that produced a magical effect upon his listener.

"I have prayed for help to come. Thank God, it was you. Bend lower, I would tell you all; but first guard against interruption by Dustin."

The stranger laughed.

"Dustin can be trusted; I have already talked with him. Fear not and speak freely."

. . . . . .

Christmas Day at Journey's End. And what a memorable occasion. The greatest day of all the year in that Virginia household. The beautiful old mansion was a picture with its polished floors where ruddy fires cast long, flickering shadows of red. Twined up the curving oaken staircase were sprays of holly and evergreen and mistletoe. Great wreaths of the same hung in every window, and the snapping logs sent their fragrance into every room.

In the dining room long tables were set—the one covered with satin damask and glittering silver and decorated china was to serve the master and his guests. Another smaller, less pretentious table was for the servants, for, following an old Scotch custom, Major Vance, in whose veins ran the blood of Scottish kings, on this one day each year feasted with his every servant and menial. The stable boys, the farm hands, even the prisoner from the guardhouse would dine on this one occasion with the master of Journey's End.

The table groaned with tempting viands—sweet Virginia ham, luscious crown roasts, game, sauces—all the delicacies of a well-stocked plantation were displayed as the guests took their places. The negroes, all except those serving the dinner, stood each at his place. Alone, pale but composed, very thin and weak, his arm in a sling, stood the highwayman. His pose was easy, though his ankles were bound together by a chain. Major Vance approached him.

"No man in chains can dine with me. Will you give me your word not to try to escape if I release you during dinner?"

"Yes," the tone was curt, and neither voice nor gaze faltered.

"Remove the chains from this man and give him a seat at my table."

There was a quick protest from Captain John, which his kinsman silenced with a wave of his hand and a brief remark: "It is my wish. He is a white man."

Anne was greatly perturbed. She sat opposite her father at the long table, and the blue satin of her gown rose and fell with tumultuous heartbeats. By what strange freak of fate had the man who had so persistently intruded upon her thoughts of late been chosen to be her guest this Christmas Day.

At her right hand sat Captain John, his dark handsome face expressing keen displeasure whenever he glanced toward where the highwayman was seated. As for the prisoner himself, he sat silently at ease while a servant carved his turkey and filled his plate. Anne stole many a timid glance at him, but aside from a low bow when first meeting her eyes, the bandit ignored her existence. He looked very tall in his black garments and white linen stock. His brown hair was brushed smoothly back and fastened in a club following the custom of the day. His face, clean shaven, revealed a well-shaped mouth and square white teeth, and his long eyelashes effectively concealed the expression in his eyes.

Once, conscious of his riveted gaze, Anne looked at him to find him reading the ancient slogan of her house, which was carved above the great fireplace:

"Vance, advance, thy will is might
In court, in forum, or in fight.
Life guards thy honor, love thy troth;
True happiness doth crown them both."

The plates were filled, the repast about to begin, when— Without was a great tramping of horses, a servant flung wide open the doors to admit two gentlemen, one tall, slender, handsome, the other vigorous, imposing. Both removed their hats. There was a murmur from all: "His Excellency!" "Lieutenant Hamilton!"

The gentlemen bowed low, the ladies bent in deep curtsy. Anne came forward to her father's side.

"General Washington," and the host of Journey's End extended a welcoming hand, "this honor and pleasure are indeed splendid. A merry Christmas to you, sir, and a dinner awaits you."

"I will partake of the dinner most gladly, Major Vance, but will be obliged to leave, perforce, immediately after. My mission is both important and secret, else I should not be traveling upon Christmas Day."

"Your pleasure, sir," and Major Vance led his distinguished guests to the table. "You know my daughter, Anne, and my sons, Andrew and Joseph.

Each greeted the venerable officer in turn.

"My niece, Mistress Mary Vaill, Captain Somers, Mrs. Leslie, Mr. Elkins, Mrs. Glass"— He stopped abruptly. He had reached the prisoner. Anne held her breath; what would follow? The highwayman had refused to give a name.

His excellency extended a hand, his face wearing one of his rare, sweet smiles. "I need no introduction to this gentleman. Capt. John Vance, I am very pleased to meet you again."

There was a moment of stunned silence; Anne saw the room reel. She watched General Washington grasp the hand of the prisoner, she was conscious of her brother Andrew's quick leap across the room, where he grappled with the man from New York, almost her fiance. She heard her father roar:

"What, sir. Do you know this man?"

"Certainly," replied His Excellency. "It is Capt. John Vance, of Albany, whom I had the pleasure of decorating for services at Minisink, and complimented him upon the great numbers of prisoners his company had captured."

Then the room reeled again, and Anne sank fainting to the floor.

She came back to the conscious world with the odor of a pungent restorative in her nostrils and opened her eyes to find herself lying upon a divan in the hall and to see Mary Vaill hovering above her. Through the open door of the dining room could be seen the diners, and Mary's voice was triumphant as she exclaimed:

"There. She is coming around nicely. I will go back to my roast duck." And without more ado she vanished.

"Anne," a voice that thrilled her spoke her name. She quickly turned her head. A handsome bronzed face was near her own, a pair of magnetic brown eyes gazed into hers. She drew back with a little gasping cry and covered her face with her hands.

"Is it true? O, what must you think of me?" she cried incoherently.

"I love you, Anne," an arm clasped her. "Look at me, sweetheart; let me read your eyes."

She gazed at him piteously.

"Whatever I did, I couldn't help it," she said slowly. He gazed a moment into her eyes, then pressed his lips to hers.

"No more could I."

After a few rapturous moments, Anne heard the whole story—how the false Captain John, who was really a renegade named Hatfield, whom he had known and to whom he had told his mission, had set upon the young officer as he journeyed through the mountains; how, while being conveyed as prisoner, John had learned not only that Hatfield intended exchanging identities with him, for he had stolen his credentials, but that by some means he had learned that General Washington was to travel the mountain defiles near Journey's End on Christmas Day. And the highwayman had planned to have his men set upon him, slay his escort, and hold the General for ransom.

Andrew Vance, while visiting the guardhouse, had recognized the prisoner, and, desiring to know the reason he had assumed the other's guilt and not declared himself, went back and stayed with him that evening after his sister had left Captain John revealed the whole truth to him, and together they planned to frustrate the kidnapping. Andrew had sent an armed posse to the place planned for the foray, and the unexpected recognition of Captain John by General Washington—something which no one had counted upon—brought about a crisis. Hatfield had been captured, as well as his confederates, and now lay under strong guard in the prison that but a few hours before had housed the man he had wronged.

The host of Journey's End came to the door.

"Will you not join us?" he asked. "I would drink his Excellency's health."

Anne and Captain John hastened forward. They once more took their places at the table.

"To General George Washington, his health and good fortune."

The toast was drunk, standing, then Lieutenant Hamilton followed with the old Virginia Yuletide wish:

"The blessings of another year be on this hearth
And on all who gather there,
Upon the master and the mistress and the guests
Who share their fare.
And here may friend and traveler find,
Forever at the Christmastide,
A welcome hand to make him ask
A blessing on this fireside."

Once more the glasses were filled. Captain John rose, every eye upon him. His handsome brown eyes found Anne's face. He turned and glanced slowly down the long line of guests.

"To Anne Vance, my beloved future wife."

He drained the glass, snapped the stem and shattered it, then before them all, amid the babble of congratulations, he took the blushing, tearful Anne in his arms and kissed her.

A RECKLESS VENTURE.
BY D. C. GALLAHER, CHARLESTON, W. VA.

On a cold day in the winter of 1864-65, I left camp near Orange Courthouse on the Rapidan River for my home in the Shenandoah Valley, on a "horse furlough." The Southern cavalryman, unlike the Northern, furnished his own horse and equipment, and when his horse became disabled, he was given a short furlough to get another one. Mine was practically on three legs, so lame that I was compelled to walk many a mile leading or driving him ahead of me.

The first night I reached Charlottesville, about thirty miles away. Realizing that my furlough was short, I trudged along as fast as I could, and with an early start the next morning, I hoped to reach my home at Waynesboro that day. It was very cold and the road was frozen, and without anything to eat for self or horse, which limped along, I keeping warm by walking most of the way. We finally reached the foot of the Blue Ridge Mountain at Afton, a station on the railroad, where a Mr. Goodloe, who was strewing fodder in his barnyard, recognized me and urged me to spend the night with him, not to attempt to cross the mountain that night, as the road was covered with ice and my horse could not walk over it, and that both of us would probably perish. I thanked him, but said: "No; I am going to see my mother to-night, sure." He gave me a pitying good-by. When I got up to the bridge over the railroad at Afton, I hesitated between scaling that ice-covered mountain road, two or three miles in distance of ascent and the same in descent, or to lead my horse along the railroad through the mile-long tunnel.

It had become very dark. I chose the latter, and my plan was to keep between the iron rails and, if I heard a train coming, to leave my horse to his fate and to run as far as I could and lie down as far away from the track as possible.

My poor horse hobbled along as fast as I could urge him, leading him in pitch darkness, and just as we emerged on the west side, I heard a freight train coming through the tunnel from the east.

After three miles more of limping along, I was under my mother's window at nearly midnight calling to her. She said she thought she was dreaming about me when she first heard my call. In a short time I was sitting by her fire, devouring a warm supper which she had hastily prepared.

This incident illustrates the hardihood and reckless chances of war which no wealth could now tempt me to face.

NOVEMBER ON AN OLD BATTLE FIELD.
BY VIRGINIA LUCAS.

The little pools of color glow
  In God, his sight;
And oak and chestnut trees arow,
  And maples dight
In yellowing crimson, fill the woods
  With amber light.

Now in late fall the grass is green
  And fields upturn
Their glittering spears of emerald sheen;
  Near by the burn,
By scattered ranks, ambrosial ragweeds yearn
  For other lands. The sun-bright fire
Has riven them of the heart's desire:
  Their spirits burn.

And delicate tints of autumn rose—
  Dogwood and vine—
Sadden the wildest longing glows;
  They, too, have known some world divine—
Or stars ashine.

But still the ash and strawberry tree
  And shellbark's gold
In radiant show and panoply
  Their cohorts hold:
While in deep pools of color, shining bright,
  Red sumac points to heaven, in God his sight.

WHEN VICKSBURG WAS BESIEGED.

(The following letter was written by Maj. W. C. Capers, of the 1st Louisiana Artillery, Gibson's Brigade, during the siege of Vicksburg, his letter being dated April 27, 1863. It is interesting to have this expression from one who was taking an active part in the defense of the then little river town, and to know how he felt about it.)

I have been placed in possession of two sheets of paper ornamented with an engraving of Vicksburg, a place that this war has rescued from comparative obscurity and invested with an interest and celebrity not inferior to the most renowned cities of ancient or modern times, and upon the fate of which the eager eyes of the whole civilized world are turned, one portion anxiously looking for and expecting its downfall, the other hoping and praying that it will withstand the shock of battle throughout the protracted and unequal contest and exhibit to the gaze of wondering millions the glorious symbol of our young Confederacy high above its battered ramparts, "torn, but flying."

Whatever may be its ultimate destiny, it has already become a place of historic prominence and will live in song and story as long as thought and language shall endure.

Unborn millions will linger in mute astonishment over the page that records the valor and heroism of her patriot defenders, even when their names shall have been lost in the rolling murmurs of the by-gone; and the hills which have rocked to the tread of a mighty soldiery and trembled beneath the roar of artillery will become invested with a classic grandeur and renown that will excite the admiration of all ages and nations, even down to the "latest syllable of recorded time."

Poetry will commemorate in heroic and undying verse the brilliant achievements of the past and the present and sigh in mournful numbers over its melancholy fall, should the fortunes of war so determine. This cruel, unnatural war has given birth to romances of deeper dye and tragedies of wilder interest than the pen of novelist ever wrote, and Vicksburg is not without her share. Some future Cooper will weave into the many-colored hues of romance these campfire experiences and throw around the unhonored graves of those who poured out their hearts' best blood in its defense that respect which is due to their memories, but unacknowledged by the world, known and felt only by the survivors of many a scene of fearful conflict.

Vicksburg is immortal, though her batteries may be dismantled and her gallant soldiers forced to retire before the countless hosts that now threaten her with destruction.

Centuries may roll away, and, like Priam's capital, its ruins may alone mark the spot of its former greatness, but, like the princes and heroes of Illium, its chief defenders will find the record of their well-doing on the page of history, which will survive the wreck of matter and invite the sympathy and admiration of all after time.

The curious traveler, or wandering philosopher, may muse amid its molding ruins, all silent, dark, and obscure, but the whole drama of its early and gigantic struggle for independence will reappear before this mental vision in all its original grandeur and sublimity; and as he cons the page that tells of those who struck so nobly and so well in freedom's holy cause, his eye will rest upon the name of none that will shine with a brighter, purer, steadier luster than that of Brig. Gen. Stephen D. Lee, Vicksburg's noblest, best, and most skillful commander.

Sketches in this department are given a half column of space without charge; extra space will be charged at 20 cents a line. Engravings $3.00 each.

Blow out, ye bugles, over the rich dead!
There's none of them so lonely and poor of old,
But, dying, has made us rarer gifts than gold.
They laid the world away, poured out the red
Sweet wine of youth; gave up the years to be
Of work and joy, and that unhoped serene
That men call age; and those who would have been,
Their sons, they gave their immortality.
—*Rupert Brooke.*

CAPT. F. G. OBENCHAIN.

Capt. Francis Gardiner Obenchain, C. S. A., known in Pemberton's army as the little "Fighting Sargent," and perhaps one of the youngest Confederate captains, passed quietly in his sleep into the Great Beyond while on a visit to his sister at Marion, Va., on October 9, 1926, at the age of eighty-three years. He was born in Buchanan, Botetourt County, Va., on February 15, 1843, and in 1875 married Anna, youngest daughter of Col. A. S. Brown, a retired banker of Memphis, Tenn. She and four daughters survive him.

Francis Obenchain was prepared in the private school of Mr. William R. Galt to enter the Virginia Military Institute, where his brother Maj. William A. Obenchain, C. S. A., was graduated in 1861, and he immediately entered the Confederate service, though but eighteen years of age, and served for the entire four years. He was the last captain to command the famous Botetourt Artillery at the siege of Vicksburg. He first won distinction at the battle of Port Gibson on May 1, 1863, when the battery with six splendid guns, which constituted the Botetourt Artillery, and of which he was then orderly sergeant, was placed in the front to be sacrificed, if necessary, in an effort to hold General Grant in check. It fired the first gun in the battle about daybreak, and soon attracted upon it the concentrated fire of two or more Federal batteries. It bore the brunt of the engagement, and, being in an exposed position, lost heavily in men, guns, and horses. At noon, the lieutenants being killed and the captain wounded, the command of the battery devolved on young Obenchain, then but twenty years of age. He was the last to leave the field late in the afternoon, and, with two guns, all that could be brought off, and which are still to be seen at Vicksburg Military Park, he rendered excellent service in covering the retreat of the Confederate troops. For this he was promoted for "distinguished valor and skill," and, at the siege of Vicksburg, commanded a force of infantry and artillery.

At the close of the war, Captain Obenchain engaged in various enterprises, but for more than forty years he was a broker in Chicago. He was an inveterate reader and student of history and possessed a remarkable memory. All of these attributes he retained to the last day of his life. When Vicksburg Military Park was laid out some years ago, he supplied much valuable information to the government, together with maps, which were accepted as authentic. One of these he had made when a lad, after the battle of Port Gibson. In recognition of his assistance, he was invited to attend the formal ceremonies at the park as a guest of the War Department.

Francis G. Obenchain was descended from a long line of American patriots who had served their country in the colonial wars and the Revolution. He was a lineal descendant of Louis Du Bois, one of the founders of New Platz, in 1660, in what is now the State of New York, and of Benjamin Borden, of Colonial Virginia. His great grandfather was one of the little band of one hundred Virginians who accompanied Gen. George Rogers Clark in the conquest of the Northwest Territory during the Revolutionary War.

At his grave in Wytheville, Va., were gathered, beside his family, the few remaining Confederate heroes who live in this locality and the loyal Daughters of the Confederacy of the Wytheville and Marion Chapters, who laid him to rest in the heart of the Blue Ridge Mountains that he had loved so well.

JOSEPH NICHOLAS THOMPSON.

Joseph Nicholas Thompson, son of Lawrence and Rebecca Brigham Thompson, was born in Franklin (afterwards Colbert) County, Ala., near what is now Barton Station, at the ancestral mansion, Mountain Home, on March 27, 1844. He died on November 13, 1926, the last of his family, having survived three sisters and a brother.

Joseph Thompson received his education at a select preparatory school near Nashville, Tenn., later entering the Montgomery Bell Military Academy of that city. When war was declared in 1861, with other comrades, he was fired with the excitement and enthusiasm for the Southern cause, and wished to volunteer in her service, but his father, being an old man, objected to his entering the army, and compromised by inducing him to attend the LaGrange Military Academy, and should the cadets be called to service, then he should volunteer and serve. When the State accepted the volunteer service of the LaGrange cadets, Joseph Thompson was one of the ten selected to assist Captain Hunt, military instructor (a West Point graduate), in drilling the new recruits who were fast assembling to fill the ranks of a regiment.

On March 12, 1862, these troops were mustered into the Confederate States army and ordered to Corinth, Miss., where the regiment became known as the 35th Alabama Infantry, Loring's Division, and the war record of Joseph Thompson follows the history of the 35th Alabama Infantry, which saw service at Baton Rouge, around Vicksburg and Jackson and Corinth, Miss.; at Kenesaw Mountain, Marietta, Peachtree Creek, and Atlanta, Ga. At the battle of Franklin, Tenn., the 35th Alabama was all but decimated, and in the charge on the breastworks Joseph Thompson was desperately wounded, taken prisoner, and sent to Camp Chase, Ohio. In the spring of 1865, he was paroled and sent to City Point, Md., for exchange; was detained at Point Lookout, Md., until June, 1865, and was finally paroled and sent South. He returned to Alabama in August, 1865, bravely determined to become an honorable, patriotic citizen.

He assisted in organizing W. A. Johnston Camp, U. C. V., and was its Commander for many years, and to the time of his death he was devoted to the memory of the Southern cause. For several years he served as brigadier general commanding the 3rd Alabama Brigade, U. C. V., and was on the staff of two Commanders in Chief. For some years he was a great, but patient sufferer. A braver, more patriotic, nobler, or more charitable spirit was never among us, for he loved and feared his God and loved his fellow man.

Maj. J. L. McCollum.

In the death of Maj. J. L. McCollum, of Atlanta, Ga., the VETERAN marks the passing of another devoted friend. He was a close friend and associate of its late founder and editor. Death came to him on December 8, 1926, after a brief illness.

Major McCollum was the oldest man in point of continuous service connected with the Nashville, Chattanooga and St. Louis Railway, his service beginnnig in July, 1871. His first railroad service began in 1866, when he was with the Willa Valley Road running from Chattanooga to Trenton, and he was later made its agent at Chattanooga. When this road was taken over by the Alabama Great Southern, he was appointed superintendent and later was master of transportation until his change in 1871. For sixty years, without the loss of a single day, he was on the roster of the Nashville, Chattanooga and St. Louis Railway, and fifty-eight of these years was as an official of the road. In November last he was honored by being elected president of the "Old Guard," the honor organization of the road, succeeding the late J. H. Latimer, who died during the year.

J. L. McCollum was born May 10, 1842, in Dade County, Ga., of Scotch ancestry. As a boy he attended the country schoolhouse built of logs. When war broke out in 1861, he enlisted for the South and became a member of the "Raccoon Roughs," a company made up of Georgia, Tennessee, and Alabama men, and commanded by John B. Gordon, later brigadier general, C. S. A. He was serving on the staff of General Gordon near the close of the war, and seven days before the surrender he was captured and sent to prison, where he remained for three months after the war was over. Major McCollum was ever faithful to the cause for which he had fought and was prominent in the association of United Confederate Veterans, serving on the staff of different Commanders in Chief from its organization.

James Walter Burns.

James W. Burns died at his home in Henderson, Ky., on April 15, 1926, at the ripe age of eighty-four years. He was born in Salem, Ky., February 16, 1842, and the next year his parents removed to Smithland, Ky., where his father died in July, 1849. Walter was then sent to the home of an uncle at Cadiz, Ky., and later went to Mississippi and made his home with an uncle there until 1857, when he returned to Kentucky. In July, 1861, he gladly offered his services to his beloved Southland, enlisting at Princeton, Ky., in Company C, 3rd Kentucky Regiment, and served faithfully and continuously until January, 1865, when he, with a number of other dismounted men, was honorably discharged at Corinth, Miss.

J. W. BURNS.

He returned to Kentucky and resumed the pursuit of farming. He professed faith in Christ in 1869, and united with the Methodist Episcopal Church, South, at Cedar Grove, later removing his membership to Bennett Memorial Church at Henderson, where he had resided since November, 1918.

Comrade Burns was married to Miss Martha Alice Sills in August, 1870, and to them eleven children were born, his wife, with three daughters and five sons, surviving him. He was a man of upright character, kindly disposition, loved by all who knew him. He was buried in his beloved gray uniform.

W. A. Rawls.

William A. Rawls was born in Tallahassee, Fla., August 26, 1851, and on December 5, at the age of seventy-five years, he sank to his eternal sleep. His service to the Confederacy was when, as a cadet of fourteen years old at the seminary west of the Suwanee, he was called to the defense of the colors of the Confederacy at Natural Bridge, Fla.

He was graduated from the Virginia Military Institute in 1872 and immediately following his graduation became a civil engineer and engaged in building a railroad east of Tallahassee, which is now the Seaboard Air Line. After serving several years as an engineer he entered the drug business in Tallahassee, in which he was very successful. He served eight years as State chemist of Florida, resigning to enter the banking business, and was elected cashier of the Capital City Bank, which institution he helped to organize. He resigned from this position to reënter the drug business in Pensacola. He retired from active business in 1920 and moved to Tallahassee; he was always active in State, county, and city politics, having served as chairman of the Democratic State Executive Committee during some of the most exciting times of Florida politics.

As a member of the legislature from Leon County for two terms, as well as city councilman of Tallahassee for a number of years, he rendered most efficient service in the interest of his county and city.

Mr. Rawls took a deep interest in the reunions of the United Confederate Veterans, and was always a very conspicuous figure at their meetings.

He is survived by his wife, a son, and four daughters.

Members of Camp Lamar, U. C. V., served as honorary guard at the burial.

George A. Hill.

George A. Hill, eighty-seven years of age, born in Bourbon County, Ky., in 1839, but a resident of Shelby County for many years, passed away on October 28, 1926, and was taken to his old home for burial. He was laid away in his uniform of gray, which he loved so well to wear at the reunions, and his casket was draped with a large Confederate flag.

In Cynthiana, Ky., at the beginning of the war, he joined the Confederate army as a member of Company D, 9th Kentucky Infantry, Orphan Brigade, with which he fought at Shiloh, Vicksburg, Baton Rouge, and other places.

On December 15, 1862, he was transferred to Company A, 9th Kentucky Cavalry, of Gen. John H. Morgan's command, and remained with that regiment as orderly sergeant until the close of the war. He was captured twice, but escaped both times before reaching prison. He was an active member of Camp John H. Waller, of Shelbyville, Ky.

[Graham Brown, Shelbyville, Ky.]

J. W. Sheppard.

J. W. Sheppard spent four years of service in the War between the States, serving as a loyal and faithful soldier of the Confederacy. He was with Company D, of the 8th Texas Regiment, Hall's Brigade, Walker's Division.

Comrade Sheppard was born in Alabama, July 18, 1841, but the greater part of his life was spent in Texas, and from that State he enlisted as a Confederate soldier. He was held in high esteem in his adopted State. He died at the home of his son near Colorado, Mitchell County, Tex., on March 15, 1926.

[His friend, E. M. McCreless, Colorado, Tex.]

JASPER N. PRATER.

After a short illness Jasper Newton Prater answered the last roll call at his home in Lake Charles, La., on May 4, 1926.

He was the youngest and last surviving member of a prominent Southwest Louisiana family, and was born October 22, 1845, in Calcasieu Parish.

Although living many years beyond the allotted span of life, scripturally speaking, he was still in the vigor of his mentality, and seemed only in his prime. No man was better known or better loved in the community, and his passing left a vacancy that will not be filled easily. A devoted husband and father, his family was deprived of a manly protector, whose constant endeavor in life had been to shield and benefit those he loved.

The community lost an eminent and patriotic citizen, devoted to the cause of liberty and progress, ever ready to respond to the call of duty, and who never failed to advocate the right and espouse the cause of the oppressed. The poor and unfortunate of any race or color always had his sympathy and help.

For thirty-five years he was a director of the First National Bank of Lake Charles, a consistent member of the Baptist Church for years, and a Mason of long standing.

In the War between the States, he served with Company I, Capt. J. W. Bryan, of the 28th Louisiana Infantry, under Colonel Landry. After the surrender, he returned to his home and, by his industry, perseverance and indomitable courage, built up a handsome competency.

On February 1, 1866, he was married to Miss Martha L. Hewitt, who died March 13, 1900. Twelve children were born to this union, of whom six sons and four daughters survive him, with his second wife, who was Miss Ida M. Mitchell, of Lake Charles.

He was a member of Calcasieu Camp No. 62, U. C. V., of Lake Charles, and his veteran comrades attended the funeral in a body. The flag-draped casket was tenderly borne to its last resting place in Orange Grove Cemetery by his six sons.

His was truly a beautiful and useful life, standing out as a beacon to the community in which he lived.

VIRGINIA COMRADES.

In reporting the deaths of two Virginia soldiers, Horace A. Hawkins, of Richmond, Va., writes that "they were good men, their records that of every real soldier. About all we can do for them now is to make this record of their service for the Confederacy, which will be of interest to their surviving comrades and valuable record for the future."

James Walter Brunet, a native of Richmond, Va., died on November 29, 1926, at his home in Petersburg, in the eightieth year of his age. He was a member of the staff of the Virginia Division, U. C. V., with rank of brigadier general.

At the age of fifteen, Walter Brunet enlisted in Company K, 32nd North Carolina Regiment, Daniels's Brigade, Rodes's Division, and served throughout the war. He was a good soldier and had a record for bravery and devotion to duty. He was well and widely known. Some forty years ago he went to Richmond from Petersburg and was made assistant foreman of the old *Richmond Dispatch*, which position he held for many years. Among the printing fraternity he was well known before the advent of the typesetting machines, being one of the masters of his trade. He was laid to his final rest in old Blandford Cemetery at Petersburg.

On November 29, in the eighty-eighth year of his age, John W. Johnston died at his home in Winchester, Va. He served as a member of Company K, 5th Virginia Infantry, Stonewall Jackson's Brigade, and was one of the men who stormed the heights at Gettysburg. Capt. George W. Kurtz, commander of the company to which comrade Johnston belonged, died a short time ago.

Comrade Johnston is survived by one brother. He was buried in Stonewall Cemetery in Clarke County, Va. His record as a soldier is one of which his comrades were proud, for he never flinched in face of the greatest dangers in the discharge of his duties.

DR. WILLIAM P. MCGUIRE.

The death of Dr. William P. McGuire at his home in Winchester, Va., in his eighty-first year, caused an unusual break in the entire medical and surgical circles of Virginia and great personal grief among the thousands who knew him and honored him, for he was truly an exceptional man—in medical and surgical renown, in business, and in all civic enterprizes, as well as a Christian gentleman, a faithful vestryman of the Episcopal Church for more than a half century, and a gallant Confederate soldier. His life was crowned with unusual honors. For many years, up to his death, he was President of the Merchants' National Bank; became president of the Medical Society of Virginia; on the boards of directors of many large enterprises, etc.; but the greatest ornament of his honored life was his conceded eminence as a surgeon. This is no wonder, for he was one of a family distinguished as surgeons, his father, Dr. Hugh H. McGuire, having many years ago established and was the head of a medical college of high rank in Washington; and his brother, Dr. Hunter McGuire, was Medical Director on the staff of "Stonewall" Jackson, who expired in the arms of his beloved surgeon, who later in Richmond became, perhaps, the most eminent surgeon in the whole South. Aside from the honors bestowed upon Dr. W. P. McGuire, he always had time and inclination, despite his onerous duties, to win and hold the affection and pride of an unusually large family connection and host of friends all over the State. His wife, who passed away some years ago, was the daughter of the late and nationallp known Hon, John Randolph Tucker.

When but a mere boy Dr. McGuire joined Chew's Battery, a distinguished command, served gallantly until the war ended, and was captured. Upon his release from prison soon after Appomattox, returning home to Winchester, he began the study of surgery and after graduation with distinction he added great luster and fame to his profession.

[D. C. Gallaher, Charleston, W. Va.]

COL. WILLIAM CARROLL VAUGHN.

A great loss has been sustained by the Chicago Camp, No. 8 U. C. V., in the passing of its beloved Commander, Col. William Carroll Vaughn. He was also the oldest member of the Camp, having reached the age of ninety-one years. He was born in Shelby County, Ky., March 16, 1835; served as a soldier of the Confederacy in Forrest's command, and was taken prisoner at the battle of Shiloh; when exchanged, he joined the Confederate cavalry under Gen. John H. Morgan.

Colonel Vaughn had been a resident of Chicago for about fifty years, and Commander of the Camp of Confederate Veterans for the past ten years or more; only three members are left. He bore the title of colonel by U. C. V. appointment. He was a writer of ability, and some of his contributions, both of prose and poetry, had appeared in the VETERAN. He was known as the oldest member of the printing fraternity of Chicago, and, notwithstanding his great age, had continued actively at work in late years. Of his nine children, three daughters survive him.

GRAY ELLIS.

On November 2, 1926, at the age of eighty-one years, veteran Gray Ellis heard the last bugle call for Taps and passed peacefully into the great beyond.

He was born in North Carolina, December 29, 1845, and went to Alabama when only four years of age, his father settling at Warsaw, a small town near Gainesville. When war was declared and companies of soldiers were being organized all over the South, Gray Ellis, then a boy of sixteen, enlisted and joined the 36th Alabama Regiment, Holtzclaw's Brigade. This company was formed at Gainesville and made up of men from all parts of Sumter County. Young Ellis served three years in the Confederate army, his services confined almost exclusively to the Army of Tennessee. He was under galling fire in many battles, notably at Resaca, New Hope Church, Chicamauga, Lookout Mountain, Missionary Ridge, Franklin, and in smaller battles. Twice wounded, he was confined in a hospital for some time with a broken leg and had to use crutches for some time afterwards.

His last illness was brought on by a fall which broke his leg below the hip, and, after being taken to the hospital, pneumonia developed and he quickly succumbed. His last request was that he be buried in his beloved gray uniform, which he had worn to many reunions and which he so loved. He was buried by the side of his beloved wife in the cemetery at Gainesville. He is survived by a son and a daughter.

Of late years, Comrade Ellis had lived in Gainesville, and at one time his home was on the site of General Forrest's surrender. When this house was destroyed by fire, he gave the land to the United Daughters of the Confederacy as a site for a monument to General Forrest, to preserve this historic spot. The marble shaft which now stands on the cliff overlooking the Tombigbee River will be a lasting memorial not only to General Forrest, but to the genial old veteran who was proud to honor with his substance the memory of a brave and beloved officer who fought so gallantly for the Southern cause.

[Mrs. Elizabeth Churchill Ward, Gainesville, Ala.]

FRANKLIN OLIVER ADAMS.

On the morning of November 14, 1926, the soul of Franklin Oliver Adams returned to Him who gave it, after a long and well-spent life of eighty-two years. He was the son of Israel and Elizabeth Adams, born September 26, 1844, in Adams County, Miss. In 1879 he married Susie, daughter of H. W. M. and Elizabeth Drake, who survives him with four sons and two daughters, also ten grandchildren.

Comrade Adams served the Southern cause in Cameron's Battery, Harrison's Brigade. He had been a life-long resident of Tensas Parish, La., living at Locust Ridge. This property was entered by his grandfather and has remained in the family. He was a most successful planter, valuable citizen, and stanch friend, charitable and kind.

Living his entire life on his ancestral home, his record has been one of unbroken success covering more than sixty years in harness. Assuming charge of the property upon the death of his father before he reached his majority, he had operated it successfully. A man of sterling worth he embodied all that made for good citizenship, enjoying the love, respect, and regard of his every acquaintance, irrespective of race, creed, or color. Possessed of personal magnetism, physical and moral courage and intellect above the average, his influence was great. Though not a Church member, he was a consistent Christian throughout his long life, attending the Methodist Church. Beneath a mound of flowers he sleeps peacefully in the Natchez cemetery.

JAMES W. REDDEN.

After a long illness, James Walker Redden died at Mokane, Mo., on October 28, 1926, at the age of eighty years. He was born near Nashville, Tenn., March 2, 1846, but had lived in Missouri since shortly after the close of the War between the States. He was a great-grandson of William Walker, a Virginian, who served through the Revolutionary War and then with his young bride went out to Tennessee, settling in Hickman County, about forty miles from Nashville, where he became one of the most influential citizens of that State. His son, William Walker, was also so loyal a sympathizer and helper of the Southern cause during the War between the States that his lands were confiscated. His daughter, Mary Walker, had married John Redden, and they were the parents of James Walker Redden, who enlisted for the Southern cause at the age of seventeen and served until the close of the war. He was with Price in the memorable last march through Missouri, and fought in the battle of Lexington.

After the war, James Redden went to Callaway County, Mo., where he was married in 1871 to Miss Sarah Janet Hays, a member of one of the oldest families of the county, and one of the best, being a direct descendant of Daniel Boone's daughter Susanna, who married W. M. Hays and lived in St. Charles County, but whose children later removed to Callaway County and were the early settlers there.

Comrade Redden was a member of the Methodist Church, a consistent Christian, and an honorable citizen in the fullest sense of the word. He led in all things for the betterment of his community. For many years he operated a large fruit orchard north of Mokane. His wife survives him with two sons and two daughters. He was laid to rest in the Mount Zion Church Cemetery, and in the funeral services every honor was accorded him as a leading citizen, and many beautiful floral tributes, the offering of friendship and love, covered the lowly mound.

DR. SAMUEL H. AUSTIN.

Dr. Samuel Hunter Austin, of Lewisburg, W. Va., died at Charleston, W. Va., on the 16th day of November, 1926, and was buried with Masonic honors from the Old Stone Church at Lewisburg, on the day following.

Dr. Austin was born in Augusta County, Va., on the 18th day of March, 1840. He was a cadet at the Virginia Military Institute, 1856-60; he attended a medical school at Winchester, Va., in 1860-61, and entered the Confederate service in June, 1861, Company B, 22nd Virginia Infantry, at Ripley, now West Virginia, with the rank of lieutenant, and was promoted to captain at the battle of Lewisburg. Later he served as assistant surgeon. He was honorably discharged about April 13, 1865, having served under Generals Wise, Floyd, Loring, and Early.

Dr. Austin located at Lewisburg at the close of the war and was married to Mary Copeland McPherson, of that place, on the 12th day of June, 1865. Later he graduated at the Medical College of Virginia, at Richmond, and then entered upon the active practice of his profession, and during his long career as a physician he was universally loved and respected and enjoyed an extensive acquaintance throughout his State.

He is survived by his wife and the following children: Mrs. W. E. R. Byrne, of Charleston, W. Va., First Vice President General, United Daughters of the Confederacy; Mrs. W. Gaston Caperton, of Slab Fork, W. Va.; Mrs. John D. Pugh, of Baltimore, Md.; Samuel M. Austin, of Lewisburg, W. Va.; Mrs. D. Meade Mann, of Richmond, Va.; E. H. Austin, of Rocky Mount, N. C.; and Mrs. G. H. Caperton, Jr., of Rush Run, W. Va.

United Daughters of the Confederacy
"Love Makes Memory Eternal"

Mrs. St. John Alison Lawton, *President General*
Charleston, S. C.

Mrs. W. E. R. Byrne, Charleston, W. Va........*First Vice President General*	Mrs. B. A. Blenner, Richmond, Va....................*Treasurer General*
Mrs. P. H. P. Lane, Philadelphia, Pa.........*Second Vice President General* 186 Bethlehem Pike	Rural Route No. 2
	Mrs. John L. Woodbury, Louisville, Ky.................*Historian General* 74 Weisinger-Gaulbert
Miss Katie Daffan, Ennis, Tex................*Third Vice President General*	Mrs. J. P. Higgins, St Louis, Mo......................*Registrar General* 5330 Pershing
Mrs. L. M. Bashinsky, Troy, Ala..............*Recording Secretary General*	
Mrs. Fred C. Kolman, New Orleans, La.... *Corresponding Secretary General* 4620 South Derbigny Street	Mrs. R. P. Holt, Rocky Mount, N. C...................*Custodian of Crosses*
	Mrs. Jackson Brandt, Baltimore, Md.... *Custodian of Flags and Pennants*

All communications for this Department should be sent *direct* to Mrs. A. C. Ford, Official Editor, Clifton Forge, Va.

FROM THE PRESIDENT GENERAL.

To the United Daughters of the Confederacy: Greeting and best wishes to each Daughter in our great organization upon the beginning of a second year of this administration.

For my reëlection to this position of trust and importance, I extend to each my sincere appreciation of the confidence thus expressed and promise my best service.

The attention of members is called to the change in officers. Those newly elected are as follows:

Second Vice President General, Mrs. P. H. P. Lane, 186 Bethlehem Pike, Chestnut Hill, Philadelphia, Pa.

Recording Secretary General, Mrs. L. M. Bashinsky, Troy, Ala.

Registrar General, Mrs. J. P. Higgins, 5330 Pershing Avenue, St. Louis, Mo.

Treasurer General, Mrs. B. A. Blenner, Box 556, Richmond, Va.

Mrs. Ramsey, former Treasurer General, U. D. C., offered her resignation at the last meeting of the Executive Committee, which was accepted. It being the duty of the President General to fill any vacancy occuring between conventions, this matter was taken up immediately with the Executive Committee and the Finance Committee, then in session, and, upon the unanimous vote for Mrs. Blenner as Treasurer General, she was duly appointed by the President General.

Attention is called to the correct address of the Treasurer General. The address is Box 556, Richmond, Va.

Those who expressed concern as to the time taken in printing and distributing the Minutes of the general convention will feel reassured at learning that the stenographic report and all reports of officers and Division Presidents and Commitees, etc., are now in the hands of the publishers, with the assurance that the Minutes will be out on February 1, according to the requirements of the By-Laws.

The Directors of the Woodrow Wilson Memorial Scholarship will serve this year in collecting the amounts pledged by Divisions in completing this fund. This will be completed by these payments and the appropriation made from the General Fund in Richmond.

The World War Records Committee was discharged, having served honorably and completed its work.

The Thomas Jefferson Memorial Foundation Committee was also discharged, being a special committee for a specific work, which was brilliantly and satisfactorily performed.

Four new committees were authorized: Committee on Proper Design of the Flag, Committee on Jefferson Davis Historical Foundation, Committee on Matthew Fontaine Maury Scholarship, Committee to Devise Plan for Securing Endowment for Oxford Scholarship.

The Richmond convention is now a matter of history. It is outstanding as one of the most brilliant and successful conventions ever held by this organization.

The Daughters of Richmond were unfailing in planning and executing those things which made the convention successful. All thanks are due them for their constant thought and devotion to the comfort and happiness of the members present.

No one in Richmond, in Virginia, or in other States, reading the accounts of the proceedings, could fail to be impressed with the vitality and power of the organization.

Year by year the women are educated in the work and become trained and efficient. The Past Presidents General are the type of women who do not feel that they have received a diploma and can remain at home and leave the work to others, but are present in force with all their experience and devotion to the cause to help in the doing of great things.

These women, as well as those on the list of Honorary Presidents and committees, are women of dignity and acknowledged social prestige, whose wish for the organization is that it may always be recognized as a body of women functioning with wisdom and dignity. To that end all things are planned, and it is hoped that each Daughter will pledge anew her loyalty and devotion to the organization, to its high aims and ideals.

Ruth Lawton.

SOCIAL FEATURES OF THE CONVENTION.

Incident to the convention of the United Daughters of the Confederacy in Richmond, Va., a very beautiful service was held at St. Paul's Episcopal Church on the morning of Sunday, November 14. After a most impressive sermon by the rector, Rev. Beverly Tucker, D.D., a Confederate flag was presented by the Daughters of the Confederacy to St. Paul's Church, in appreciation of its splendid Confederate history. One had but to recall that here both General Lee and President Davis worshiped, and that here centered many sacred memories of that time, to feel the spirit of such a service.

Crowded into the week that followed were so many pleasant and interesting events, and so many varied social features, that to attempt to give an account of all of that part of the convention would be to fill many pages of the Veteran.

The week's social program had its beginning with the President's dinner on Monday evening. The Flemish room of the Jefferson Hotel was beautifully decorated with red and white roses, as were also the long tables. Place cards were in the form of little folders, showing on the inside an engraving of the White House of the Confederacy and on the opposite page the poem "Virginia." During the dinner, Miss Alfreda Peel, of Salem, Va., in costume of the sixties, sang charmingly many Southern folk songs and old ballads collected from the mountains of Virginia and North Carolina. Mrs. St. John A. Lawton, President General, was guest of honor, and Mrs. A. C. Ford, President of the Virginia Division, was hostess.

The local convention committee, Mrs. Charles E. Bolling, chairman, was hostess on Tuesday to the President General and other U. D. C. officers at a luncheon, which was a most enjoyable affair. On Tuesday afternoon, Richmond's four D. A. R. Chapters—the Commonwealth, the William Byrd, the Chancellor Wythe, and the Nathaniel Bacon—gave a reception to the convention and all visiting D. A. R.'s at the Mayo House. These hostesses left nothing undone that would contribute to the pleasure of their guests. The rooms were beautifully decorated, the music was lovely, and their hospitality most enjoyable.

Immediately following the short program of welcome on Tuesday evening in the auditorium, a reception to the entire convention was held in the parlors of the Jefferson Hotel. This was a most brilliant assemblage and one that will long be remembered. The receiving line, which extended almost the entire length of the parlors, began with the President General, the general officers, the Past Presidents General, and ended with the Division Presidents. Even the spacious floors of that magnificent hotel were taxed to the utmost to accommodate the crowd.

Some pleasant social affair was planned for the officers and guests every day during the week. One of the most delightful of these affairs was the luncheon given by Miss Sally Archer Anderson at her home on Franklin Street on Wednesday.

The Colonial Dames gave a tea for U. D. C. officers and all visiting Dames on Wednesday afternoon, and the Woman's Club entertained the convention at their beautiful club on Friday afternoon.

As it is the custom to take one entire afternoon for recreation and play, Thursday was the day upon which centered much of interest. Beginning with a luncheon given at the Confederate Home by the Sons of Veterans, the afternoon was a continuous round of sight-seeing and pleasure. Interesting addresses were made by the hosts of the luncheon, and a thoroughly enjoyable musical program was rendered during the meal by a negro quartet. Immediately afterwards, guests were taken for an automobile ride, the course of which included a visit to Hollywood Cemetery, St. John's Church, the Battle Abbey, and many points of historic interest. Later the members of the various Divisions were entertained at teas in their honor at many of the lovely and hospitable homes in the city. The only regret was that it was impossible for one to attend all these pleasant functions.

The ballroom of the Jefferson Hotel was the scene of the annual Pages' Ball on Friday evening. This is one of the most pleasant events of the convention, and each year the wonder grows how so many beautiful and charming girls can be found. Surely no more beautiful group has ever graced a ballroom floor than the pages of this convention.

Another feature of the convention which is always looked forward to with pleasure is the Jefferson Davis Highway Dinner. This year, under the able management of Mrs. John L. Woodbury, chairman of the Highway Committee, it was held in the Palm Room of the Jefferson and was a memorable event. Among the speakers was Col. Warren Jefferson Davis, of California, who, it will be remembered, received a Cross of Service at the Hot Springs convention of 1925.

The War Directors' dinner, with Mrs. P. H. P. Lane as hostess, was also most pleasant.

A fitting close for a week of brilliant entertaining was the reception given by Gov. and Mrs. Harry Flood Byrd at the Executive Mansion on Saturday afternoon, the last day of the convention. The stately old Mansion looked very lovely, and there was a feeling that nowhere was more genuine Virginia hospitality dispensed than here. Governor and Mrs. Byrd were assisted in receiving by the President General, her officers, the Past Presidents General, and the President of Virginia Division.

Following the close of the convention, on Sunday a pilgrimage was made to Williamsburg, where service was held in old Bruton Church, followed by luncheon at William and Mary College. Later the journey was continued to Jamestown Island, and there under the shadow of the old church tower and within the confines of that historic shrine, another service was held. Dr. Goodwin, of William and Mary College, conducted both services.

U. D. C. NOTES.

Arkansas.—A most successful convention of the Arkansas Division was held at Arkadelphia. The Ladies' Library Building, where the meetings were held, was beautifully decorated with flags, flowers, and Southern smilax, and was filled to capacity at each session by interested delegates and visitors.

An interesting feature of the convention was the book, "History of Arkansas's Part in the War between the States, and the Days of Reconstruction," which, fresh from the press, was displayed for the first time and offered for sale.

Encouraging reports were made by officers and chairmen of committees and showed much progress along all lines of work. Particularly was this noticeable in scholarships taken, loan funds increased, and in the number and quality of essays submitted.

An hour was given to the Margaret Rose Children of Confederacy Chapter of Little Rock, and their little President, Elizabeth Walker, read their splendid report.

Mrs. George Hughes, of Benton, was elected Division President to succeed Mrs. Lora Goolsby, of Fort Smith, the beloved retiring President.

Kentucky.—The annual convention of the Kentucky Division, was held in Hopkinsville and Fairview, Ky., October 20, 21, 1926. The Chapters of these two towns were joint hosts, the first day's session being held in Hopkinsville and the second day's session at Fairview, the birthplace of President Davis.

Mrs. John L. Woodbury, Historian General, gave a most interesting address on Jefferson Davis, Secretary of War, on Historical Evening. Hon. Pat Harrison, of Mississippi, visited the conventon and spoke regarding the life of President Davis. The President's report showed progressive work, three new Chapters having been organized, and one new C. of C. Chapter formed at Lexington with twenty-six members. The Kate M. Breckinridge Chapter, of Danville, received a prize of a beautiful loving cup for securing the most new members based on percentage of enrollment. The W. N. Bumpus Auxiliary of the C. of C., Owensboro, received a medal given for most new members. Mrs. J. Harris Baughman, of Danville, presented the President with a gavel made from wood taken from the battle field at Perryville, Ky. Louisville will entertain the 1927 convention.

* * *

Missouri.—The dedication of the Liberty Memorial, a monument erected by the people of Kansas City in memory of the heroic dead of the World War, was perhaps the greatest event in the history of Kansas City. One hundred and fifty thousand persons attended the dedicatory exercises and heard the address given by President Calvin Coolidge, who, with Mrs. Coolidge, was a guest of the city for the day. The members of Camp No. 80 U. C. V., were invited to attend the exercise and were given splendid seats. Gen. A. A. Pearson, Commander of the Missouri Division, U. C. V., and Mrs. Pearson, were among the six hundred guests who attended a luncheon at the Hotel President in honor of President and Mrs. Coolidge. The members of Camp No. 80 and a number of the members of the five Chapters U. D. C. were invited to be on the reception committee to welcome Queen Marie of Rumania and her children, who were also guests of the Memorial Committee in the evening. Queen Marie extended greetings and placed a wreath upon the monument in the name of the king of Rumania. It is with appreciation that the members of the U. D. C. acknowledge the kindness of the memorial committee in thus honoring the Confederate veterans upon this eventful occasion.

At the annual reunion of the Missouri Division, U. C. V. held in Kansas City, October 1, 2, Gen. A. A. Pearson was reëlected State Commander. General Pearson is the typical Southern soldier and gentleman.

Mrs. James S. Eldredge entertained the Stonewall Jackson Chapter, of Kansas City, with a luncheon on November 15. Mrs. J. B. Robinson was honor guest. A happy diversion in the program was the presentation of a birthday cake to Mrs. Allen L. Porter by the Chapter President, Mrs. Robert W. Smith. Mrs. Porter responded with cordial words of greeting to the members.

A most interesting souvenir, in the scrapbook of the R. E. Lee Chapter of Blackwater, is a picture of the George B. Harper Camp of Confederate Veterans, taken when they and their wives were guests of the R. E. Lee Chapter at a picnic last summer at Chateau Springs. Mrs. Bernard C. Hunt, State President, and Mrs. E. C. Hunt, Past State President, were guests.

Mr. H. J. Gorin, of the Confederate Home at Higginsville, sends a most interesting account of an entertainment given recently at the Home. About one hundred and fifty guests assembled to enjoy the program, prepared and supervised by Mrs. M. C. Duggins, of Slater, Mo., who is chairman of the "Men and Women of the Sixties." Mrs. Duggins is familiarly known at the Home as "Our Virginia." An excellent program was given by artists who accompanied Mrs. Duggins from her home town. Mrs. Charles Schmidt, Rocky Moore, and Mrs. Vermillion rendered a number of familiar songs with repeated encores, which were greatly appreciated. Mrs. Chambers, matron of the Home, assisted the committee in serving refreshments during the evening. Mrs. Smitherman thanked the visitors in behalf of the women of the Home for their kindness in bringing so much cheer to them.

* * *

Virginia.—Recently, in one of our daily papers, a very pathetic story was printed about a veteran at the Confederate Home in Richmond who, fearing he would have no flowers on his casket, and loving them so, bought a little bunch of artificial flowers and requested the Superintendent to place them on his coffin when he died.

Lee Chapter, U. D. C., was so touched by the story, and, fearing there might be other gray-clad warriors who loved flowers also and longed for them at their funeral, the Chapter decided to place flowers on every casket which otherwise would go without them. We consider this token of our love and affection for the veterans of the Home a rare privilege for service.

The Chapter will also give the veterans and the women at the Confederate Home a dinner during the Christmas holidays. This is in addition to the regular monthly entertainments given both "Homes."

New members are coming in at every meeting, and the Chapter is active in all work of the Virginia Division.

William Calmes Black, the only man in Montgomery County, Md., to ask to be transferred from a practically exempt class in order to volunteer, was the first recipient of a Cross of Service at the hands of Arlington Chapter, of Clarendon Va. The Chapter made it a memorable occasion, inviting the Camp of S. C. V. to unite with them at their meeting in November, at which time the decoration was bestowed, and also having as their guests the American Legion of the town and the Legion Auxiliary.

The Adjutant of the Sons, Mr. R. B. James, was master of ceremonies, and Commandant French made a brief address explaining the meaning of the Cross. Mrs. C. C. Moffatt, the Chapter President, had a few words to say, and Miss Margaret Rees, the Legion's representative at Philadelphia and a former President of Arlington Chapter, C. of C., made the presentation. The C. of C. Chapter, of which Mr. Black's small daughter is secretary, furnished an interesting program of music and recitations, and Mrs. Lloyd Everett, Third Vice President of the Virginia Division, U. D. C., paid a tribute both to the recipient of the Cross and to his grandfather, Capt. William C. Black, through whose service the award was made, and ending with the recitation of an original poem, "The Service Cross." In her remarks she stated that Captain Black, who served the Confederacy as Chief of the Foreign Supply Office of the Trans-Mississippi Department, had been so successful in getting cotton through the blockade, both by ship to the West Indies and wagon trains to Mexico, and in bringing in supplies—not one of his ships or wagon trains ever having suffered capture—as to earn from President Davis the title of "The most useful man in the South," while his enemies bore testimony to his untiring and successful activity by expressly exempting him from the general amnesty after the cessation of hostilities and confiscation of all his property. Two of his letterpress books, believed to be among the very last official records of the Confederacy, were presented by his granddaughter to the Confederate Museum a few years ago. Eleven of his sixteen grandsons served in the World War, and Arlington Chapter, Children of the Confederacy, owes a fourth of its membership to his great-grandchildren.

* * *

West Virginia.—The twenty-eighth annual convention of the West Virginia Division was held in historic Shepherdstown on September 21-23, with a good attendance. Shepherdstown's reputation for hospitality was fully sustained, and every minute was enjoyed to the utmost.

The most important work of the convention was a complete revision of the State constitution and by-laws.

The hearts of all were saddened to learn of the death of Miss Orra Tomlinson, the former State Historian, which occurred in May at her home in Charles Town. Miss Tomlinson held the office for years and made such a wonderful Historian that she and her work will never be forgotten. A special memorial service was held for her at the Memorial Hour.

The main feature of Historical Evening was the reading of extracts from an unpublished book, "Personal Recollections of a Young Confederate Soldier," by the late Henry Kyd Douglas, of Stonewall Jackson's staff. The extracts dealt with the history of Shepherdstown and its vicinity, and were read by John Kyd Beckenbaugh, a nephew of the author.

A most delightful reception was held on the evening of the

21st at Bellvue, the magnificent colonial home of Mrs. Minnie Reinhart Ringgold. Quite an attraction at the reception was a real old-time negro mammy, Aunt Sallie Stubbs, leaning on her cane at the head of the stairway to greet the ladies when they went to remove their wraps.

At the close of the convention automobiles were provided for a ride over the Antietam battle field, and to the monument on the banks of the Potomac erected in honor of James Rumsey, the first man to invent and successfully sail a boat by steam.

The meeting next year will be in Hinton.

The following officers were elected: President, Mrs. B. M. Hoover, Elkins; First Vice President, Mrs. Edwin Robinson, Fairmont; Second Vice President, Miss Sallie Lee Powell, Shepherdstown; Recording Secretary, Miss Loretto Keenan, Clarksburg; Corresponding Secretary, Miss Anna Feamster, Alderson; Treasurer, Miss Mary Calvert Stribling, Martinsburg; Historian, Mrs. John C. Dice, Lewisburg; Registrar, Mrs. Nelle Huneke, Charleston; Director Children of the Confederacy, Mrs. Charles L. Reed, Huntington; Custodian Crosses of Honor, Miss Maria Vass Frye, Keyser; Honorary President, Mrs. F. J. Manning, Charles Town.

* * *

Oklahoma.—Officers of the Oklahoma State Division elected in 1926 are: President, Mrs. Hettie Work, Durant; First Vice President, Mrs. George Dismukes, Chickasha; Second Vice President, Mrs. R. Roy Evant, Oklahoma City; Third Vice President, Mrs. Minnie Sawyer, McAlester; Fourth Vice President, Mrs. H. A. Wakefield, Tulsa; Recording Secretary, Mrs. Count Dunaway, Shawnee; Corresponding Secretary, Mrs. E. J. Bray, Henryetta; Treasurer, Mrs. Victor Cochran, Tulsa; Registrar, Mrs. Fred Morris, Antlers; Historian, Mrs. L. A. Morton, Duncan; Recorder of Crosses, Mrs. Carrie I. Jones, Sayre; Custodian of Flags, Mrs. W. E. Durham, Oklahoma City; Auxiliary Director, Mrs. W. T. DeSpain, Enid; Chaplain, Mrs. G. H. Hester, Muskogee; Parliamentarian, Mrs. T. F. Gorman, Bartlesville; State Editor, Mrs. C. A. Galbraith, Ada.

* * *

South Carolina.—The many friends of Capt. M. M. Buford, of Newberry, were distressed to know that for the first time since the organization of the State fair he was not able to attend this year, owing to his continued illness. It was at Captain Buford's suggestion that free admission had been granted to Confederate veterans each year. He has been ill since February and was unable to attend either the State reunion of veterans or the general reunion for the first time in their history and has been greatly missed by his comrades.

In the county of Orangeburg there lives possibly the most remarkable woman in the State of South Carolina. To begin with, she has celebrated her ninety-ninth birth anniversary, which in itself is a remarkable fact; then a fact that is of more particular interest to all lovers of the Confederacy is that she is, perhaps, the only living woman in the State who had a husband and two sons in the Confederate service. She is Mrs. Olivia Pooser. Although she has passed many milestones along life's journey, Mrs. Pooser does not dwell too much on the past, but lives very decidedly in the present. Indeed, so modern is this woman, now nearing the century mark, that she voted in the election of 1924. She is an honorary member of Paul McMichael Chapter and is still active enough to attend meetings.

She proudly wears a "Bar of Honor" presented by the Confederated Southern Memorial Association to mothers of the Confederacy, and has attended two State reunions within recent years.

Tennessee.—Mrs. A. R. Dodson, of Humboldt, Historian of the State Division, has gotten out a handsome booklet for the Historical Department, in which she stresses the study in State history in addition to the general course of study in the organization for the Daughters and Children of the Confederacy. A list of the "Days of Abservance" is given also a list of the prizes offered by the State Division and the rules of contest. The booklet is handsomely illustrated, and a credit to the Division.

WOMEN OF THE CONFEDERACY.

The VETERAN has received reports of the passing of a number of our dear Confederate women of late, mothers and wives who had a part in the war through their sacrifice and devotion to the Confederate cause no less noble than that of their sons or husbands. Mention is here made of several who have died within the past month or so.

Mrs. Cornelia A. Yerger, widow of Col. Edward M. Yerger, of Jackson, Miss., died at the home of her daughter, Mrs. W. G. Curd of Saverton, Mo. Readers of the VETERAN will recall the interesting reminiscences contributed by her in the VETERAN for December, 1924. She had passed into her ninety-fifth year. Interment was in Greenwood Cemetery, Vicksburg, Miss.

Mrs. Louise Samira Hartsfield, wife of Col. J. M. Hartsfield, Commander of R. E. Lee Camp, of Fort Worth, Tex., died in that city at the age of eighty-one years. A little more than sixty years of happy married life had been theirs, and both were in their eighty-second year. Her husband and only brother served in the same company of the 17th Mississippi Regiment, Barksdale's Brigade, and the brother was killed in one of the last battles of the war.

THE SERVICE CROSS.

BY CATHERINE C. EVERETT.

"The brave give birth to the brave."—how true
This bit of garnered wisdom of the years.
The men in gray, who wrote in blood and tears
Their country's saddest, yet most glorious, page,
Have left to us a mighty heritage
Of fortitude, of flaming courage high,
Of valorous deeds, and names that will not die
While time shall last; and then—they left us you.

Manning, Lejeune, and York—the list would grow
Too long if we should try to name the ones
Whose valor brightened the World War—the sons
And grandsons of the men who followed Lee.
But we rejoice that all the world could see
How, when the long roll sounded, Dixie gave,
Gave swiftly, gladly of her sons—the brave
Unto the brave give birth, this truth we know.

With crosses twain we point our heroes' worth;
Bronze Honor Cross for veterans of the gray,
Gold Service Cross for you, their sons, to-day,
And write your record with that matchless host,
That deathless band, the South has honored most,
And gladly honors now, afresh, to-day
In you, their sons, as pridefully we say:
"The brave unto the brave *have* given birth."

Confederate Veteran.

Historical Department, U. D. C.

MOTTO: "Loyalty to the truth of Confederate History."
KEY WORD: "Preparedness." FLOWER: The Rose.
MRS. JOHN L. WOODBURY, *Historian General.*

HISTORICAL STUDY FOR 1927.

GENERAL TOPICS: THE CONFEDERATE CONGRESS.

U. D C. Program for January.

The historical program for this year will take up the members of the Confederate Congresses. Each month the State Historians will have a general article in the VETERAN dealing with the State's representatives.

It is hoped that this program will bring to light some hitherto unrecorded history. The U. D. C. membership is requested to look up all old diaries, any memorial books which may have been printed by the families of these men.

It will not be an easy matter to get the facts in regard to all of them, but we must remember that all of the history of the Confederacy was not made on the battle field. The Congress which carried on the government, their plans and policies, their struggles, economic and political, will be the object of our research this year.

PROVISIONAL CONGRESS.

First Session.—Assembled at Montgomery, Ala., February 4, 1861. Adjourned March 16, 1861, to meet the second Monday in May.

Second Session (called).—Montgomery, Ala., April 29, 1861. Adjourned May 21, 1861.

Third Session.—Richmond, Va., July 20, 1861. Adjourned August 31, 1861.

Fourth Session (called).—Richmond, Va., September 3, 1861. Adjourned same day.

Fifth Session.—Richmond, Va., November 18, 1861. Adjourned February 17, 1862.

PERMANENT CONGRESS (FIRST).

First Session.—Richmond, Va., February 18, 1862. Adjourned April 21, 1862.

Second Session.—Richmond, Va., August 18, 1862. Adjourned October 13, 1862.

Third Session.—Richmond, Va., January 12, 1863. Adjourned May 1, 1863.

Fourth Session.—Richmond, Va., December 7, 1863. Adjourned February 17, 1864.

PERMANENT CONGRESS (SECOND).

First Session.—Richmond, Va., May 2, 1864. Adjourned June 14, 1864.

Second Session.—Richmond, Va., November 7, 1864. Adjourned March 18, 1865.

(In the following list of names of representatives from the States "P" indicates the Provisional Congress, and 1 and 2 the First and Second Permanent Congresses.)

South Carolina seceded December 20, 1860.

Senators: Robert W. Barnwell, 1, 2; James L. Orr, 1, 2.

Representatives: R. Barnwell Rhett, P; Robert W. Barnwell, P; Lawrence M. Keitt, P; James Chestnut, Jr., P; Charles G. Memminger, P; William Porcher Miles, P, 1, 2; Thomas J. Withers, P; William W. Boyce, P, 1, 2; James L. Orr, P; Milledge L. Bonham, 1; John McQueen, 1; James Farrow, 1, 2; Lewis M. Ayer, 1, 2; William D. Simpson, 1, 2; James H. Witherspoon, 2.

PROGRAM FOR CHILDREN OF THE CONFEDERACY 1927.

In addition to the questions and answers each month, we will make a number of historical tours through the South, so each member of the C. of C. is asked to trace a map of the United States on a piece of cotton cloth with India ink. Make the map about two feet wide and a foot and a half high. Do this in January, and we will mark the tours with colored pencils later.

All places are to be located on the map and something about them put in the notebooks.

JANUARY.

Mark Fort Sumter. What did President Lincoln promise in regard to sending supplies here? Did he keep his word? Was this an act of war? Read "Kree," by Armistead C. Gordon. Library of Southern Literature, Volume V, 1911.

Catechism on Confederate States of America, based on "U. D. C. Catechism for Children," by Mrs. Cornelia Branch Stone (1912), revised and enlarged (1926) by Miss Decca Lamar West in honor and loving memory of Mrs. Cornelia Branch Stone.

Questions and answers will be printed each month, and it is hoped that every member of a Chapter of Children of the Confederacy will memorize all of them.

1. What causes led to the War between the States from 1861-65?

The disregard on the part of the States of the North for the rights of the Southern States.

2. How was this shown?

By the passage of laws annulling the rights of the people of the South, rights that were given to them by the Constitution of the United States.

3. What were these rights?

The right to regulate their own affairs, one of which was to hold slaves as property.

4. Were the Southern States alone responsible for slavery?

No; slavery was introduced into the country in colonial times by the political authorities of Great Britain, Spain, France, and the Dutch merchants, and in 1776, at the time of the Declaration of Independence, slavery existed in all of the thirteen colonies.

5. How many of the colonies held slaves when the Federal Constitution was adopted in 1787?

All except one.

6. Did slavery exist among other civilized nations?

Yes; in almost all; and our mother country, England, did not emancipate her slaves until 1843, when Parliament paid $200,000,000 to the owners.

7. After the first introduction of slavery into the colonies, how was the African slave trade kept up?

By enterprising ship owners of New England, who imported the slaves from Africa and secretly sold their cargoes along the coast, after the States of the North had abolished slavery.

8. Why did not slavery continue to exist in the States of New England?

Because it was found unprofitable, and they sold their slaves to the States of the South.

NOTE TO DIRECTORS.—Chapter directors will please enlarge upon the action of the colonies in regard to the slave trade, also explain why the indictment of King George in regard to the same was left out of the final draft of the Declaration of Independence.

U. D. C. PRIZES FOR 1927.

The Raines Banner.—To the Division making the largest collection of papers and historical records and doing the best historical work.

Youree Prize, $100.—Awarded by Cross of Service Committee to Division directors on a per cent and per capita basis.

Jeanne Fox Weinmann Loving Cup.—To the Division reporting the greatest amount of historical work done in its schools. Annual competition.

Blount Memorial Cup.—To the Division bestowing the greatest number of Crosses of Service during the year. Annual competition.

Alexander Allen Faris Trophy.—To the Division registering the greatest number of U. D. C. members between the ages of eighteen and twenty-five. Annual competition.

Orrin Randolph Smith Medal.—For the best report of a Jefferson Davis Highway director.

ESSAYS (WRITTEN BY MEMBERS OF U. D. C. CHAPTERS).

Rose Loving Cup.—For best essay on Confederate surgeons and hospitals.

Anne Sevier Loving Cup.—Given by the three daughters of Gen. T. K. Churchill—Juliette C. Hankins, Emily C. Califf, Mattie C. Langhorne—for best essay on "The Right of Secession." Annual competition.

Mrs. John A. Perdue Loving Cup.—For the best essay on home life behind the lines: substitutes for food, clothing, etc.

Hyde-Campbell Loving Cup (formerly *Hyde-Campbell Prize*) —For best essay on poetry of the South.

Twenty-Five Dollars.—Offered by Mrs. Bessie Ferguson Cary, of Virginia, for best essay on "Mosby's Rangers," a memorial to her father, Rev. Sydnor G. Ferguson, one of Mosby's men.

Twenty-Five Dollars.—Offered by Miss Mary D. Carter, Virginia, to U. D. C. member selling greatest number of copies of Horton's Youth's History.

Anna Robinson Andrews Medal.—For best essay on "The Confederate Peace Conference" in Washington, February, 1861.

Roberts Medal.—For second best essay submitted in any contest.

Martha Washington House Medal.—For the best essay on Gen. Albert Sidney Johnston.

RULES.

1. Essays must not contain over two thousand words. Number of words must be stated in top left-hand corner of first page.

2. Essays must be typewritten, with fictitious signature. Real name, Chapter, and address must be in sealed envelope, on outside of which is fictitious name only.

3. Essays must be sent to State Historian, who will forward to Historian General by October 1, 1927.

4. Essays on all subjects given may be submitted, but only two on each subject can be forwarded by State Historians.

5. Prize winning essays to be property of the U. D. C.

6. These same rules apply to essays submitted by C. of C.

C. OF C. PRIZES.

Robert H. Ricks Banner.—To the C. of C. Chapter that sends in the best all-around report.

The Grace Clare Taylor Loving Cup.—Given by Mrs. Charles S. Wallace to the general organization to be presented to the C. of C. Chapter registering the most new members during the year.

Anna Flagg Harvey Loving Cup.—Given by Mrs. J. P. Higgins in memory of her mother. To the Division director who registers the greatest number of new members in the C. of C. Annual competition.

Florence Goalder Faris Medal.—To the Division director who registers the second highest number in the C. of C. Annual competition.

Mrs. W. S. Coleman Loving Cup.—To be offered to the Chapter director who places the greatest number of books in school libraries. Books on Confederate history to be used as supplemental reading. Annual competition.

ESSAYS.

Mrs. J. Carter Bardin.—Five dollars in gold to the boy or girl of Confederate lineage, between the ages of ten and twelve, for best essay on "Arkansas Soldiers of Gen. Sterling Price's Command." In memory of her grandfather, Henry L. Cordell, an Arkansas volunteer.

Mrs. May Avery Wilkins, Seattle, Washington.—Five dollars in gold for best essay on "Causes of the War between the States." Open to students west of the Mississippi, between ten and twelve years old.

Mrs. Bennett D. Bell.—In honor of her black mammy, Matilda Cartwright, five dollars in gold to the C. of C. member writing the best essay on "Mammy in the Old Plantation Days." Preference will be given to paper giving incidents which have never been in print. Contestants will give authority.

AN ANNUAL CELEBRATION.

The following comes from Capt. John L. Collins, of Coffeeville, Miss.:

"On the 10th of November, the Yalobusha Chapter of the Mississippi Division, United Daughters of the Confederacy, gave the veterans, wives, and widows their annual feast. For many years past they have been reminding us that we have a warm place in their hearts for the four years spent in our younger days in repelling the invaders of the sacred domain which our fathers established. The day was auspicious for such an occasion. There were eight veterans, ranging in age from eighty-two to ninety years, all full of that spirit of patriotism which had inspired their young manhood sixty years ago, and which has never been 'downed.'

"Thirty-five years ago, E. C. Walthall Camp, No. 1301, U. C. V., was organized at the old historic county seat of Coffeeville, Miss., and named in honor of that general famous at the period just a century ago. And on April 6, 1862, in the battle of Shiloh, she gave six of her leading citizens in an hour's time, which in the annals of history should be observed. One of these distinguished men, Col. A. K. Blythe, under the administration of President Buchanan, was minister to Spain. Lieut. Col. D. L. Herron, Capt. F. M. Aldridge, Lieut. Whitfield Morton, Capt. George Hairston, Capt. Joseph Caldwell, and James Bellamy, a handsome, gentlemanly soldier, whose father was a wealthy planter, were the other heroes. Thus it was that Coffeeville paid, in that battle alone, a ransom that deserves special mention when the historians verify and give to future generations the story of the martyrs of our glorious cause of 1861-65.

"The Coffeeville Daughters displayed an unusual effort in all the arrangements for making the day memorable in every way. Handshaking came as the joyous 'capstone' to end the day's proceedings, with a 'God bless you. We hope to see you present next year at our annual convocation.' And so mote it be."

Confederated Southern Memorial Association

MRS. A. McD. WILSON............................*President General*
   209 Fourteenth Street, N. W., Atlanta, Ga.
MRS. C. B. BRYAN......................*First Vice President General*
   1640 Peabody Avenue, Memphis, Tenn.
MISS SUE H. WALKER.........*Second Vice President General*
   Fayetteville, Ark.
MRS. E. L. MERRY...*Treasurer General*
   4317 Butler Place, Oklahoma City, Okla.
MISS DAISY M. L. HODGSON....*Recording Secretary General*
   7909 Sycamore Street, New Orleans, La.
MISS MILDRED RUTHERFORD.................*Historian General*
   Athens, Ga.
MRS. BRYAN W. COLLIER..*Corresponding Secretary General*
   College Park, Ga.
MRS. VIRGINIA FRAZER BOYLE.........*Poet Laureate General*
   653 South McLean Boulevard, Memphis, Tenn.
MRS. BELLE ALLEN ROSS...........................*Auditor General*
   Montgomery, Ala.
REV. GILES B. COOKE.............................*Chaplain General*
   Mathews, Va.

STATE PRESIDENTS

ALABAMA—Montgomery.....................Mrs. R. P. Dexter
ARKANSAS—Fayetteville ....Mrs. J. Garside Welch
WASHINGTON, D. C.........................Mrs. D. H. Fred
FLORIDA—Pensacola.....................Mrs. Horace L. Simpson
GEORGIA—Atlanta......................Mrs. William A. Wright
KENTUCKY—Bowling Green..........Miss Jeane D. Blackburn
LOUISIANA—New Orleans.................Mrs. James Dinkins
MISSISSIPPI—Greenwood............Mrs. A. McC. Kimbrough
MISSOURI—St. Louis.........................Mrs. G. K. Warner
NORTH CAROLINA—Asheville.................Mrs. J. J. Yates
OKLAHOMA—Oklahoma City........Mrs. James R. Armstrong
SOUTH CAROLINA—Charleston............Miss I. B. Heyward
TENNESSEE—Memphis.....................Mrs. Mary H. Miller
TEXAS—Dallas.............................Mrs. S. M. Fields
VIRGINIA—Richmond.......................Mrs. B. A. Blenner
WEST VIRGINIA—Huntington.........Mrs. Thomas H. Harvey

All communications for this Department should be sent *direct* to MRS. MARY FORREST BRADLEY, *Editor*, 2043 Cowden Avenue, Memphis, Tenn.

NEW YEAR'S GREETING.

Again, my dear coworkers, through Divine Providence, I am permitted to send you most affectionate greetings and cordial good wishes in the dawning of the new year, 1927, and to bid you Godspeed in your efforts to perpetuate, to carry on, this "our bounden duty and service," in the same loyal spirit which has in all these years since 1865 animated and encouraged the older associations, which we point to with pride as the oldest patriotic organization of women in America. Columbus, Richmond, Atlanta, Memphis, Montgomery, and others flung their banner to the breeze way back in 1865, and have stood in *unbroken* line each year in paying tribute to our immortal heroes of the sixties.

As Methodism dates back to John Wesley, so the Memorial Associations began with Columbus, Ga., leading, and other States rapidly falling into line until the whole South rose *en masse* in beautiful tribute on our Southern Memorial Day. With heartfelt sorrow we realize that a few of our charter Memorial Associations, which entered into the Confederation in 1900, have fallen by the wayside, victims to the new order of things seemingly, unconscious of the fact that in so doing they were selling their birthright, forgetful of the heritage bequeathed them by their own mothers. The Southern Memorial Day is ours by inheritance. A chartered organization, national in its scope and by the spirit of the devoted Southern mothers who conceived the idea, we pledge anew, on the threshold of another year, our best efforts to sustain the sacred trust which they have reposed in us, pursuing our way in the quiet dignity befitting the descendants of the gentlewomen of the old South.

With pride in your constancy, with joy in your steadfastness, and congratulations upon your achievements, I again wish you each and every one a new year of increased activity, of peace and happiness in every home and fireside, and I pray God's richest blessings on you in this new year, which is full of promise to all that diligently seek.

Yours in loving service,

MRS. A. McD. WILSON, *President General, C. S. M. A.*

C. S. M. A. NOTES.

In writing of her inability to attend the meeting of the Confederate Memorial Association at the Marietta Golf Club, on November 17, Mrs. R. L. Nesbit, of Atlanta, Ga., tells of the memories brought up in that connection, saying:

"How that sacred name, Memorial Association, recalls the vivid past, how many dear faces rise before me in the vista of bygone years, and how gladly would I join in recalling scenes and struggles when our Marietta Memorial Association, with the help of Kenesaw Chapter, U. D. C., was waging what we often feared was a losing fight to reclaim and beautify our long-neglected and desolate Confederate cemetery. We hadn't a dollar in our treasury, and brave hearts were needed to undertake the stupendous task; but that forlorn waste, gradually yielding to the encroachments of broom sedge, persimmon, and sassafras bushes, appealed to every sentiment of gratitude and patriotism. There over three thousand soldiers had been removed from Chickamauga battle field and from all along the line of the Western and Atlantic Railroad, under the devoted direction of Miss Green and Mrs. Williams, of Columbus, Ga., by State enactment, and with aid from the State of Georgia. Here rest in their last grim sleep soldiers not only from Georgia, but from every Southern State, including Maryland and Missouri, having made their last stand in defending Georgia soil and Georgia homes.

"Gen. William Phillips always stoutly maintained that ours, the Marietta Memorial Association, was the first to celebrate the 26th day of April after it had been declared the legal holiday. Be that as it may, since that first celebration, there has been no break in the record. Even in the terrible days of Reconstruction, when the struggle for rehabilitation, for even existence, was being fought by a stricken and impoverished people, that lonely spot was never forgotten. Each 26th day of April would witness the memorial service, sometimes by only a few devoted members, when a hymn was sung and a prayer was offered under the canopy of heaven—if raining, under a tent or other temporary awning—and with such flowers as could be gathered from desolated gardens. But gradually the State of Georgia seemed to forget its obligations, and it remained for our Association to step into the breach and reclaim this desolate spot. That we accepted the trust and filled the obligation, let the history of that time testify. Sewers were put in; drainways repaired; every unsightly bush removed; shrubbery planted; the whole place sodded in grass; a marble headstone placed for each waiting soldier; a speaker's stand of brick and marble built; also a marble gateway and fountain; and, lastly, a peerless monument. Then the little cannon captured from the cadets of the Georgia Military Institute, so long a prisoner in New York, was brought home and stands guard on the brow of the hill just across from the site of the Military Institute, which was burned by Sherman's soldiers. The Marietta Golf Club house now stands on this spot."

The Memorial Association of Marietta, Ga., recently entertained at luncheon at the Golf Club. The honor guests were Mrs. A. McD. Wilson, President General, C. S. M. A., and many other distinguished guests, including Gen. J. C. Lynes, honorary member. At the close of the luncheon, Mrs. Lyon, President of the local organization, was presented with a memorial pin.

OUR WOMEN IN THE SIXTIES.

In reading the following story, one can realize the wonderful strength and tenacity of the Confederate troops when having such women back of them, even though facing odds of four to one in troops thoroughly equipped and having the world at large to draw upon for additional men, while the Confederates had only their own people to supply their necessities, and with a country surrounded by a blockade so drastic that it was almost a miracle for people or commodities to "pass through the lines." Mrs. M. R. Lyon, of Marietta, Ga., gives this interesting account of the resourcefulness and energy of one brave Southern woman during those terrible four years and her undaunted courage in the face of almost impossibilities:

"In 1863, my brother, Capt. Sam Y. Harris, was in Virginia with Longstreet's Division. A fellow soldier of his command, going home on furlough, offered to take any message to Captain Harris's family at their home, 'Noon Day,' about seven miles from Marietta, Ga.

"The message Captain Harris sent was for a new suit of clothes. You can imagine the consternation this request must have caused his devoted family. There was no cloth to be bought, as everything had been used for uniforms months before. The soldier comrade would return in a week's time to carry the package to Captain Harris. There was no time to be lost, for he must not be disappointed. What did these splendid, indomitable people do, exemplifying the true spirit of the unconquerable South? His father had the sheep that were grazing in the meadow brought to the yard and sheared, while Mrs. Harris, with the assistance of her daughter, Mrs. Jim Latimer, and a faithful servant carded and spun the wool into yarn and wove it into cloth, then dyed the goods, and, with wonderful skill and patience, made it into a suit of clothes for their dear soldier at the front—all within a week's time.

"That is the spirit of our grand old Southland, and it is with us yet!"

Mrs. Lyon also mentioned some of the many substitutes used during those times of stress and anxiety when the real thing could not be procured. Ink was made out of ink balls, and she says that it was better ink than we had in this late war. Tea of dried raspberry leaves; coffee of parched rye, ground and boiled. No sugar came into the South toward the latter days of the war, but sorghum syrup was used and found not a bad substitute. Home-made candles were fine, made of tallow and beeswax. A curious dip called "Betties" were useful and easy to make, the wick being wrapped around a stick, though one had to be careful that the stick did not catch on fire while the wick was burning. Salt was very scarce, and often it was necessary to dig up the earth in smokehouses, dripping it like lye and boiling it down until only salt remained. Beautiful straw hats were made of dried shucks, which were plaited and sewed together. When prettily lined, they were very becoming to the fresh young faces, whose owners were proud to wear them.

Homespun dresses, the thread dyed with a decoction of barks from the woods near-by, adorned lithe young bodies and matronly figures, all woven and made at home. When a "store-bought" dress was brought to light from the depths of some old treasure chest or trunk, what rejoicing there was. Its valuable material was used only as trimming, or buttons were covered with it, showing resplendent on a garment of far humbler origin.

A book could be filled with accounts of the ingenuity and endurance of the Southern women during the war under privations so bravely borne, and the spirit of sacrifice which gave courage to the heart and strength to the arm of our Confederate soldier, who was never conquered, but—outnumbered!

A MESSAGE FROM THE EDITOR.

My Dear Coworkers: As 1927 is ushered in, may we not rededicate ourselves to the perpetuation of the work so nobly begun by our sainted mothers and grandmothers? What you are doing in your Association is of interest to others, so I am relying on your aid in making our memorial page one of interest, knowledge, and inspiration.

Cordially, MARY FORREST BRADLEY, *Editor.*

RETURN OF THE COLORS.

An interesting and touching incident connected with the annual Memorial service in the Confederate section of Arlington Cemetery was the return of an old flag which had been carried by "Mosby's Men." A few of those men were present at the services, and the flag was presented to Capt. Frank M. Angelo as the representative of the old command, and when the last survivor of that famous band shall have passed away, the colors will be placed in the Battle Abbey at Richmond, Va., with other sacred and historic relics of the Confederacy.

This old flag had seen service. It was "made and presented by the ladies of Mosby's Confederacy, Fauquier, Loudoun, and Fairfax Counties, 1863," and was to be "preserved as an incentive to the valorous spirit of the fighting youth of a united nation." Bunting was a scarcity in those days, and the blue field of this flag had been cut from the blouse of a Union soldier; the red stripes are of fair quality bunting, while the white stripe is of unbleached cotton. But it was an emblem of the loyalty and devotion of Southern women, and as such it was cherished by Mosby's men, under sacred promise that its colors should lead only to victory

At the close of the war the flag was hidden by Captain Whitescarver, who afterwards entrusted it to Capt. Harry Hatcher. It passed in turn to Capt. Fountain Beatty, and it last went to Lieutenant Dorsey, of Company C, who at his death left it to his son to be cherished as a sacred trust. This son, George Maynard Dorsey, now of New York City, kept it in a safe deposit vault from 1907 to 1926, when he took it to Washington and presented it to the survivors of the old 43rd Battalion, men who had followed it through the war and fought under it at Sharpsburg, Winchester, and Kernstown, practically the entire Valley Campaign, under the leadership of Stonewall Jackson, Ewell, Early, and A. P. and D. H. Hill. The few survivors present were moved to tears when Captain Angelo recalled the original presentation over sixty-three years before; none of them had seen the flag since the close of the war.

After the flag was received by Captain Angelo, followed by the United States Military Band, he led a procession around the Confederate monument, all the spectators taking part—an inspiring sight.

Sons of Confederate Veterans

LUCIUS L. MOSS, COMMANDER IN CHIEF, LAKE CHARLES, LA.

GENERAL OFFICERS.

WALTER L. HOPKINS, Richmond, Va............*Adjutant in Chief*
JOHN M. KINARD, Newberry, S. C..............*Inspector in Chief*
JOHN A. CHUMBLEY, Washington, D. C....*Judge Advocate in Chief*
DR. W. H. SCUDDER, Mayersville, Miss..........*Surgeon in Chief*
V. R. BEASLEY, Tampa, Fla...............*Quartermaster in Chief*
MAJ. E. W. R. EWING, 821 Southern Building, Washington, D. C.
Historian in Chief
B. T. LEONARD, Duncan, Okla..............*Commissary in Chief*
REV. H. M. HALL, Johnson City, Tenn..........*Chaplain in Chief*

EXECUTIVE COUNCIL.

LUCIUS L. MOSS, *Chairman*..................Lake Charles, La.
N. B. FORBES, *Secretary*........................Atlanta, Ga.
CHARLIE M. BROWN...........................Asheville, N. C.
SUMTER L. LOWRY................................Tampa, Fla.
EDMOND R. WILES...........................Little Rock, Ark.
JUDGE EDGAR SCURRY......................Wichita Falls, Tex.
JESSE ANTHONY, 7 Iowa Circle.............Washington, D. C

DEPARTMENT COMMANDERS.

CHARLIE M. BROWN, Asheville, N. C..Army of Northern Virginia
SUMTER L. LOWRY, Tampa, Fla...............Army of Tennessee
EDMOND R. WILES, Little Rock, Ark., Army of Trans-Mississippi

DIVISION COMMANDERS.

DR. W. E. QUIN, Fort Payne......................Alabama
DR. MORGAN SMITH, Little Rock..................Arkansas
JOHN A. LEE, 208 North Wells St., Chicago, Ill...Central Division
ELTON O. PILLOW, 2413 North Capitol Street, Washington, D. C.
District of Columbia and Maryland
SILAS W. FRY, 245 Central Park West, New York, N. Y.
Eastern Division
JOHN Z. REARDON, Tallahassee......................Florida
DR. W. R. DANCY, Savannah.........................Georgia
J. E. KELLER, 1109 Fincastle Road, Lexington....Kentucky
JOSEPH ROY PRICE, 419–20 Giddens-Lane Building, Shreveport, La.
ROBERT E. LEE, 3124 Locust Street, St. Louis.....Missouri
JOHN M. WITT, Tupelo...........................Mississippi
J. D. PAUL, Washington......................North Carolina
L. A. MORTON, Duncan, Okla.......................Oklahoma
A. D. MARSHALL, 1804 L. C. Smith Building, Seattle, Washington
Pacific Division
RED ELKINS, Greenville.......................South Carolina
J. L. HIGHSAW, Memphis...........................Tennessee
LON S. SMITH, Austin................................Texas
R. G. LAMKIN, Roanoke...........................Virginia
E. L. BELL, Lewisburg........................West Virginia

All communications for this department should be sent direct to J. R. Price, Editor, 419–20 Giddens-Lane Building, Shreveport, La.

ANNUAL DUES AND OTHER INTERESTS.

PAY ANNUAL DUES AND RECEIVE CERTIFICATE.

Walter L. Hopkins, Adjutant in Chief, S. C. V., says that the experience of the Divisions during the past few years has shown that the most progressive Camps secure the dues of their old members before the first of the year, thereby enabling them to devote their efforts during the year to the securing of new members and the real work of the Sons of Confederate Veterans.

Collect at once all Camp dues ($1 for old members, $2 for new members) and remit to Walter L. Hopkins, Adjutant in Chief, 609–615 Law Building, Richmond, Va. As soon as dues are received, individual membership cards, engraved in four colors, will be sent for distribution to the members paying.

The next convention of the Sons of Confederate Veterans will be held in Tampa, Fla., April 5–8, 1927. The railroads have already granted a *reduced rate* to the members of our organization. The certificates, which will enable a member of the Sons to purchase a ticket at the reduced rate, will be issued only to the *paid-up members* and "Official Ladies" of the Confederation. Individual membership cards will be issued by general headquarters only upon the receipt of dues from the Camp. Admittance to the social functions of the convention and the registration at the convention headquarters, which will entitle the members and delegates to badges, will be limited to the paid-up members who hold the 1927 membership cards, issued by general headquarters.

A fifteen-day excursion to Havana, Cuba, leaving Tampa on the 7th and 10th of April, has been secured for *bona fide* members of the Sons of Confederate Veterans and the members of their families at a greatly reduced rate. Hundreds of Sons will take advantage of this excursion. Further details of the excursion will be sent you at a later date.

It is suggested that you begin at once a campaign to increase the membership of your Camp. Begin now to collect and remit the 1927 dues on all old members so that you can devote the time between January and the convention in securing new members.

MEMORIAL TO PRIVATE HECTOR W. CHURCH, COMPANY H, NEW YORK HEAVY ARTILLERY, U. S. A., 1864–65.

In his native town of Oxford, Chenango County, N. Y., there died in July, 1920, an old Union veteran of the War of 1861–65, who left a most noteworthy will. This will, executed May 29, 1920, gave his old home to an old friend, a small legacy to another friend, and "all the rest, residue, and remainder of my property . . . to the Daughters of the Confederacy." This Society was instructed to use a certain part of said residue "toward perpetuating the fame of four Confederate heroes: 'Jefferson Davis, Gen. Robert E. Lee, Gen. John B. Gordon, Gen. Jubal Early, . . . and the residue as they deem best'"—an instruction which the Daughters of the Confederacy have doubtless carried out wisely and well, as is their wont.

This will and its spirit and purpose so aroused the admiration of a comrade of Washington Camp No. 305, Sons of Confederate Veterans, that he suggested to some personal friends that a copy of the "Recollections and Letters of Gen. Robert E. Lee," by his son, Capt. R. E. Lee, Jr., be bought by subscription, because it represented most truthfully the best in the South, and be sent to the Oxford Memorial Library and there be deposited and dedicated to the honor and the memory of Hector W. Church. This suggestion started a movement to honor this Northern admirer of some of the great leaders of the South, and the response was so prompt and so cordial that not merely one volume but some fifty or sixty valuable books and pamphlets were soon bought and have been sent to Oxford as the foundation of the Memorial, and contributions are still going forward and will continue to go.

These books, moreover, are already doing their work of realizing an often-expressed wish that lay very near General Lee's heart, the wish that sectionalism might pass away and reconciliation might draw near between North and South on the basis of good citizenship and kindly feeling.

AN OLD PLUG OF TOBACCO.

Capt. Roby Brown, of Shouns, Tenn., as gallant a Confederate as ever led men to battle, at a Confederate reunion in Bristol, Tenn., was presented with a very unique and interesting souvenir by the mayor of that city. It was an aged piece of plug tobacco, manufactured by hand, and with it was this memorandum:

"This piece of tobacco was made by the Reynolds Tobacco Company, of Winston-Salem, N. C., in 1856, and was on its way to the Federal government to be distributed to the Federal soldiers when it was wrecked near Glade Springs, Va., in 1863, on the property of one Mr. W. M. Byars, who claimed the government owed him for right of way of the railroad, which they had taken over, and when the train was wrecked he took his negroes and carried off a large quantity of cotton goods and about 3,000 pounds of tobacco.

"The tobacco was hidden in the attic and walls of the home and was not discovered until 1924, or sixty-eight years later.

"The stamps on the boxes show this tobacco is seventy years old, and is given you as à souvenir by one Mr. N. H. McClellan, of Glade Springs, Va., who is a third cousin of General McClellan, of the Federal army, and whose own father was a Confederate soldier stationed at Saltville, Va., to protect the salt works during the war."

PATRIOTIC ANCESTRY.

One of the Sons who addressed the veterans at the meeting in Port Arthur, Tex., has a particularly illustrious ancestral war record. He was St. Clair Favrot, Baton Rouge, La., Past Commander, Louisiana Division of the Sons of Confederate Veterans. Favrot had a great-grandfather in the American Revolution, a grandfather in the War of 1812, several uncles in the Mexican War, and his father shouldered a Confederate rifle in the War between the States; and just to prove that he was worthy of that noble lineage, Favrot himself was a member of the United States fighting forces in the Spanish-American unpleasantries.

Favrot is secretary of the Louisiana tax commission.

CAMP NOTES.

Officers for 1927 of Camp Sterling Price, St. Louis, Mo., are: Commander, Joseph Mullen; First Lieutenant Commander, Norman L. Lincoln; Second Lieutenant Commander, Edward C. Fisher; Adjutant, William L. Ross, Jr.; Treasurer, J. W. Estes; Quartermaster, Cortez Kitchen; Historian, M. N. Davis; Color Sergeant, Chilton Atkinson; Chaplain, R. B. Gibson.

* *

The W. D. Simpson Camp, of Laurens, S. C., was issued a charter on November 11, 1926. H. Y. Simpson was elected Commander, and W. D. Ferguson, Adjutant. Other members of the Camp are: S. C. Owens, W. P. Hudgens, C. H. Roper, C. H. Casque, J. C. Todd, Albert C. Todd, J. A. Franks, R. E. Hughes, and S. W. Deen.

* * *

The Charlie Crockett Camp, at Wytheville, Va., was recently organized. J. L. Porterfield is Commander; the Adjutant is John W. McGavock, Jr. The other members of the Camp are: R. C. Patterson, John W. Robinson, James M. Graham, Thomas E. Simmerman, J. M. Kelly, John T. Wassom, Rev. F. J. Brooke, Jr., W. H. Simmerman, Curran F. Sanders, H. M. Hauser, and David S. Blair.

* * *

The William E. Jones Camp was recently organized at Abingdon, Va. S. F. Hurt was elected Commander, and J. G. Penn, Adjutant. The applications of the following members were approved: Alex Stuart, John M. Litton, W. Y. C. White, G. I. Miller, R. J. Summers, M. H. Davidson, E. C. Hamilton, Dr. F. H. Smith, Dr. P. S. Smith, Dr. J. C. Motley, I. B. Wells, C. J. Brown, C. C. Wright, G. G. Preston, R. K. Lowry.

THE IDEAL OF A STATE.

What constitutes a state?
Not high-raised battlements or labored mound,
 Thick wall, or moated gate;
Not cities proud, with spires and turrets crowned;

 Not bays and broad-armed ports,
Where, laughing at the storm, rich navies ride;
 Not starred and spangled courts,
Where low-born baseness wafts perfume to pride.

 No—men, high-minded men,
With powers as far above dull brutes endued,
 In forest, brake, or den,
As beasts excel cold rocks and brambles rude;

 Men, who their duties know,
But know their rights, and, knowing, dare maintain;
 Prevent the long-aimed blow,
And crush the tyrant, while they rend the chain—

 These constitute a state;
And sovereign law, that with collected will
 O'er thrones and globes elate,
Sits empress, crowning good, repressing ill.

 Smit by her sacred frown
The fiend dissension like a vapor sinks;
 And e'en the all-dazzling crown
Hides his faint rays, and at her bidding shrinks.
—*Sir William Jones.*

TWO FAMILIES OF OCTOGENARIANS.

A letter comes from Mr. Graham Brown, of Shelbyville, Ky., inclosing a clipping in regard to three brothers Mitchell, Confederate veterans, whose combined ages total 253 years, all being in the eighties. These brothers—G. W. Mitchell, aged eighty-one; Joseph Mitchell, aged eighty-five; and Nathan Mitchell, aged eighty-seven—all entered the Confederate army from Trigg County, Ky., but the two first named now live in Louisville.

Thinking he could "equal or beat that record," Mr. Brown says: "I called on Mr. Isaac Garrard Marksburg, of this city, who is eighty-eight years of age, and learned that his two brothers, who were with him in the Confederate army, are still living. John Emerson Marksburg, of Emerson, Mo., is eighty-six years old, and William H. Marksburg, of Nevada, Mo., is eighty-four years old, their combined ages being 258 years. I regard these as two very find family records."

Comrade A. C. Burnett, of Cadiz, Ky., also writes about the Mitchell brothers, and adds an interesting little incident in connection with the service of Joe F. Mitchell, who "was badly wounded at the battle of Jackson, Miss., and reported dead. A card was pinned on a dead soldier with Mitchell's name on it, and this man was buried at Lauderdale Spring, Miss., and on the grave stone was the name of 'J. H. Mitchell, 8th Kentucky.' With a card on him bearing the name of the dead soldier, Mitchell himself was sent to Mobile with a number of badly wounded men. His family and friends mourned him for quite a while as dead, but he is very much alive yet. At this same battle of Jackson, he rescued a ten-year-old girl from a house in the line of battle which had been struck by shell several times, and at the reunion in Atlanta a few years ago he met this girl, then a gray-haired woman."

A CONFEDERATE CEMETERY.

With one bright lane of native pines
Mild art is here content;
A simple slab each grave defines—
No more has beauty lent.

But some one filled with Southern pride,
Among the rest has led
A shaft with this sweet thought supplied!
"To the Unknown Dead."

The soldier who this grove supplied,
That buried here might be
The Southern dead, now sleeps beside
His "buried chivalry."

PEMBERTON'S CAVALRY.

A writer in the *Columbus* (Ga.) *Ledger* brought out the fact that the late Dr. John D. Pemberton, pioneer druggist of Columbus, was the originator of the famous Coca-Cola drink, which has made the fortunes of other people, as he sold the formula.

Dr. Pemberton was engaged in the drug business in Columbus when, in June, 1864, he organized Pemberton's Cavalry, in which were enrolled a number of the pioneer residents of that community, and he served with that organization through the remaining months of the War between the States. The organization was commanded as follows: Captain, J. D. Pemberton, first lieutenant, J. A. Frazier; second lieutenant, A. G. Redd; third lieutenant, H. L. Thomas; first sergeant, John Sanders; second sergeant, J. L. Biggers; third sergeant, B. A. Clark; first corporal, L. J. Biggers; second corporal, Charles Spear; and the following enlisted men: W. H. Brays, Ben Bethune, J. J. Cox, J. C. Cook, Sr., Ben Culpepper, Ed Culpepper, J. D. Carter, A. A. Chapman, J. H. Ennis, Able Edge, John Fuller, Cash Fisher, Robert Green, L. D. Gray, S. S. Hughes, B. W. Howard, M. T. Hollis, William N. Jones, H. L. Jones, William A. McDougald, Edward McLaran, Jerry Massey, Hiram Massey, William J. McBryde, Sr., William J. McBryde, Jr., William Munn, A. Morrison, Jep Morrison, LaFayette Morrison, William Nunnally, John Osborne, William Parkman, John Powers, Seab Parker, George Sapp, Sandy Sapp, George Schley, Robert E. Stockton, Richard Taliaferro, Z. A. Willis, Robert Willis, M. C. Wooten, George White, Daniel Williams, W. E. Wardlaw, John Wardlaw, Woolfolk Walker, Daniel Wynne, and Mort Weems.

This data was secured from Judge R. J. Hunter, of Columbus, now eighty-six years young. If any of the members are now living, it would be interesting to have an account of the service of this cavalry command.

A GRANDMOTHER'S AUTHORITY DURING THE WAR.

BY D. C. GALLAHER, CHARLESTON, W. VA.

Almost every one can recall his dear, good grandmother's indulgence and her imperious authority when asserted in his childhood especially, if not later. The scene and instance here recorded were at a Southern lady's home in the Shenandoah Valley of Virginia, soon after the close of the War between the States. Several gentlemen from the North, sitting upon the porch overlooking the lawn, were enjoying a recital by my brother of the battle on March 2, 1865, at Waynesboro, Va., in which he recalled how the Yankees, after driving the Confederates out, had galloped over the lawn, flower beds, etc., of our mother and captured a dozen or more prisoners there.

Now, all of her life our mother was wont to sit in her room at the window, looking out upon her flowers while she was reading, sewing, or crocheting, and when we, her little children, while playing, would trespass upon her flowers or shrubbery, she would give a warning or threatening tap upon the window with her thimble or crochet needle, which was straightway heeded by our scampering away. This tradition of the authority of that thimble-tapping signal was handed down to her grandchildren, who always respected it. So in the midst of this war recital by my brother, a little grandson eagerly listening, inquired: "Uncle Charley, didn't grandmother tap with her thimble on the window at the soldiers running over her flowers?"

The little fellow supposed that of course and instantly, General Sheridan would have called a retreat of his whole army if grandmother had only tapped on the window!

COMMENDS HORTON'S "HISTORY OF THE WAR."

In the following, Gen. Morris Schaff, whose book on "Jefferson Davis, His Life and Personality," gave him wide favor in the South, commends the republication of Horton's "Youth's History of the War." Writing to Miss Mary D. Carter, who sponsored the republication of this book, he says:

"I was truly glad to hear that your undertaking of bringing out Horton's History had been so successful. The South, and especially your dear old Virginia, owes you a debt of gratitude for what you have done in throwing the light of truth on the cause for which so many fell. Yes, I'm truly glad you have been rewarded for carrying on your battle, almost alone, against the defamers of your homeland.

"*The great myth, planted and nourished by the Republican Party, is fast losing its leaves*, and I predict that more of them will fall on the coming out of Beveridge's 'Life of Lincoln.' I knew him slightly, and he is an opinionated man; but in his talk he has given me the ground for my expectation.

"Of course, use anything that will help you in my 'Life of Davis,' who ultimately will stand out as the first gentleman of his day."

NEGRO STORIES AND SAYINGS.

Rev. Dr. Henry M. Wharton has been requested to compile the stories and sayings of the old-time negro of the South as far as they may be gathered from all sources.

Dr. Wharton, having been born in Culpeper County, Va., in the year 1848, his father a slave owner, was reared among the negroes of the plantation, and, is, therefore, familiar with their dialect.

He is the compiler of "War Songs and Poems of the Southern Confederacy," and is, at this time, one of the chief officers of the United Confederate Veterans.

It is his request that any reader of this notice, who can recall any story or saying of the negroes of the Old South, will kindly send it to him.

His address is 224 West Lafayette Avenue, Baltimore, Md.

B. T. Clark, of Tupelo, Miss., is so interested in the VETERAN that he plans to have his children and grandchildren keep up the subscription after he is gone, and if other veteran subscribers would make the same provision for the VETERAN'S future, it would be assured. Try to get the young people interested now.

WILLIAM and MARY QUARTERLY
HISTORICAL MAGAZINE

Published by the College of William and Mary, Williamsburg, Virginia

EDITORS

J. A. C. CHANDLER
President William and Mary College

E. G. SWEM
Librarian William and Mary College

The purpose of the *QUARTERLY* is to print new information relating to the history of Virginia

Subscription, $4.   ISSUED QUARTERLY   Single Copy, $1.

ONLY A DUD.

While he was making his way about his platoon one dark night, a sergeant heard the roar of a "G. I. can" overhead and dived into a shell hole. It was already occupied by a private, who was hit full in the wind by the noncom's head. A moment's silence—a long, deep breath, and then—

"Is that you, Sarge?"

"That's me."

"Hot dog! I was just waiting for you to explode."—*Everybody's.*

DOUBTFUL HONOR.

Ceredo, W. Va., has a strange history. The town was started by some mistaken Abolitionists, who felt that the way to get away from slavery was by planting colonies in the South. Ceredo was first selected for that purpose by the noted philanthropist, Eli W. Thayer. It is situated where the Big Sandy River empties into the Ohio. It makes a present adventure into the news columns by Mr. and Mrs. Lott M. Wellman establishing a record of five sets of twins and thirteen children in their married life of thirty-six years. Mr. Wellman is fifty-seven and his wife fifty-three.—*National Tribune.*

A NEW PLANT.—"Yes," the teacher explained, "quite a number of plants and flowers have the prefix 'dog.' For instance, the dog-rose and dog-violet are well known. Can any of you name another?" There was silence, then a happy look illuminated the face of a boy at the back of the class. "Please, miss," he called out, proud of his knowledge, "collie-flowers!"

These cuts show both sides of our Marker for Confederate Graves. It is made from the best grade of iron, weighs 20 pounds, measures 15x30 inches, painted black or gray, and approved by the General Organization, U. D. C.

PRICE, $1.50 EACH

F. O. B. ATTALLA

ATTALLA FOUNDRY AND MACHINE CO.
Attalla, Ala.

Deafness
From All Causes, Head Noises and Other Ear Troubles Easily and Permanently Relieved!

Thousands who were formerly deaf, now hear distinctly every sound—even whispers do not escape them. Their life of loneliness has ended and all is now joy and sunshine. The impaired or lacking portions of their ear drums have been reinforced by simple little devices, scientifically constructed for that special purpose.

Wilson Common-Sense Ear Drums often called "Little Wireless Phones for the Ears" are restoring perfect hearing in every condition of deafness or defective hearing from causes such as Catarrhal Deafness, Relaxed or Sunken Drums, Thickened Drums, Roaring and Hissing Sounds, Perforated, Wholly or Partially Destroyed Drums, Discharge from Ears, etc. No matter what the case or how long standing it is, testimonials received show marvelous results. Common-Sense Drums strengthen the nerves of the ears and concentrate the sound waves on one point of the natural drums, thus successfully restoring perfect hearing where medical skill even fails to help. They are made of a soft sensitized material, comfortable and safe to wear. They are easily adjusted by the wearer and out of sight when worn. What has done so much for thousands of others will help you. Don't delay. **Write today** for our FREE 168 page **Book on Deafness**—giving you full particulars.

Wilson Ear Drum Co., (Inc.) in Position 395 Todd Bldg., Louisville, Ky.

THREE THOUSAND YEARS OLD.

It is officially announced that an oak tree, cut down during the demolition of the historic Wingerworth Hall, Derbyshire, was at least 3,000 years old, weighed 15 tons, measured 18 feet round the butt, and had a first branch six feet in girth.

Wood from this tree is being used in work at the ancient parish church of Bakewell, celebrated for its association with the Manners family, including the famous Dorothy Vernon, who eloped with Lord Manners.—*Canadian American.*

Hubby (at golden wedding).—"Well, dear, all the years have flitted by, and I haven't deceived you yet, have I?"

Wifie.—"No, John, but goodness knows you've tried hard enough."—*Answers.*

DON'T WEAR A TRUSS

BE COMFORTABLE— Wear the Brooks Appliance, the modern scientific invention which gives rupture sufferers immediate relief. It has no obnoxious springs or pads. Automatic Air Cushions bind and draw together the broken parts. No salves or plasters. Durable. Cheap. Sent on trial to prove its worth. Beware of imitations. Look for trade-mark bearing portrait and signature of C. E. Brooks which appears on every Appliance. None other genuine. Full information and booklet sent free in plain, sealed envelope.

BROOKS APPLIANCE CO., 211 State St., Marshall, Mich.

DAUGHTERS OF DIXIE

UPON the Daughters of the South devolves an obligation as sacred as high heaven---an obligation to keep ever before her children the lofty ideals or chivalry for which the South has always stood. It is she alone who must instill in them a reverence for the heroic men and for the patriotic memories of a 'storm-cradled nation.' The broadest duty to her country demands this service at her hands. As the divinely appointed guardian and teacher of the young, it is to her that the youth of the South must look for instruction."

"AMPLITUDE of KNOWLEDGE" for a vital duty

"It is the duty of the Daughter of the South to inculcate Southern truths at the home fireside; and to supply her with the necessary means for performing this task with thoroughness the LIBRARY OF SOUTHERN LITERATURE has been provided. It should appeal to her as no other work has ever done or can ever do. Why? Because it reflects the innermost soul of the South. It reveals the wealth of thought, of sentiment, and of character by which the Cavalier race has ever been distinguished. It constitutes the fullest, the strongest, and the most complete defense of our people which has ever been made at the bar of public opinion. There is no sinister sectionalism reflected, our thoughts are centered on sectionalism as it relates to home and interest and affection for one's neighbors."

LIBRARY OF SOUTHERN LITERATURE, within its seventeen volumes, by each of its 8,000 pages, furnishes history, traditions pressed through its Literature. It should become the treasure of each household, the beacon light for our children, and does perpetuate the contributions of the South in American letters.

FILL OUT AND MAIL TO-DAY FOR OFFER TO THE VETERAN'S READERS

THE MARTIN & HOYT CO., PUBLISHERS, P. O. Box 986, Atlanta, Ga.

Please mail prices, terms, and description of the LIBRARY OF SOUTHERN LITERATURE to

Name..

Mailing Address..